GROWING UP
CHRISTIAN

JIM MARIAN

VICTOR BOOKS ®
A DIVISION OF SCRIPTURE PRESS PUBLICATIONS INC.
USA CANADA ENGLAND

**To
my parents,
Edward and Darlene Marian**

**whose faith led me to Christ,
whose example I have tried to follow,
whose love and support I constantly receive.**

Thank you.

Scripture quotations, unless otherwise indicated, are from the *New American Standard Bible,* © the Lockman Foundation 1960, 1962, 1963, 1968, 1971, 1972, 1973, 1975, 1977. Quotations marked (NIV) are from the *Holy Bible, New International Version,* © 1973, 1978, 1984, International Bible Society. Used by permission of Zondervan Bible Publishers. Quotations marked (NKJV) are from *The New King James Version,* © 1979, 1980, 1982, Thomas Nelson, Inc., Publishers.

Copyediting: Lin Johnson, Jane Vogel
Cover Design: Mardelle Ayres
Cover and Interior Illustrations: Gary Locke

Library of Congress Cataloging-in-Publication Data

Marian, Jim.
  Growing up Christian / by Jim Marian.
      p.   cm.
  ISBN 0-89693-802-6
  1. Teenagers—Religious life. 2. Church work with teenagers.
I. Title.
BV4531.2.M3595   1992
259′.23—dc20
                                                                91-31087
                                                                       CIP

1   2   3   4   5   6   7   8   9   10   Printing/Year   96   95   94   93   92

Names of actual persons, living or dead, have been changed to protect their privacy. Several personal accounts contained herein have been fictionalized.

Contents

25362

Acknowledgments

Thanks to my beautiful wife, Lynne,

> My partner in life and in ministry whose constant encouragement is my greatest source of joy and strength. Her editing skills, valuable insights, and critical evaluation of the manuscript helped shape and produce these pages.

Thanks also to my brothers in the ministry with whom I have had the privilege of serving alongside in the high school department at First Evangelical Free Church in Fullerton, California:

> Doug Haag, whose character I truly admire
>
> Eric Heard, whose encouragement keeps me going
>
> John Hoppis, whose servant heart ministers to me
>
> Jack Hawkins, whose creativity inspires me
>
> Dave Enns, whose love for kids is an example to me
>
> Craig Deane, whose zeal for ministry motivates me

"Iron sharpens iron, so one man sharpens another" (Proverbs 27:17).

Thank you to my Lord and Savior Jesus Christ.

Foreword

Julie came up to me after I spoke at her Christian high school assembly and said, "I don't have an exciting testimony. I've never been abused and I love my mom and dad. I can never remember a time when we didn't go to church. Sometimes I wish I had a conversion like a few of my friends. My faith is so boring."

My eight-year-old daughter told me recently that she wants to be either a youth worker, a television evangelist(!), or a spy. Last week she didn't want to go to Sunday School because "it's boring." She said, "I already know all about Isaiah."

Yes, there are definitely joys, stresses, and challenges of working with what Jim Marian calls the "born believer. Marian has given us great wisdom and insight on young people who have "grown up" Christian, and he has helped us deal with the specific struggles that tend to emerge from a Christian home.

Jim Marian is the perfect person to write this book. He grew up in a Christian home, he has worked with hundreds of students from Christian homes, and he has a depth of understanding of the important issues in the church, youth ministry, and this ever-changing youth culture. Putting aside the subject of growing up Christian, this is just a great youth ministry text. Not only does Marian deal with issues few youth ministry books have focused on—such as faith development and apathy—he also has put together an outstanding section on discipleship strategies for ministry. This book is extremely well researched and brings cutting-edge substance to youth ministry.

Although I read the book primarily with youth workers in mind, my wife picked it up and immediately said, "This is a must-read for Christian parents." Once again we are reminded that youth ministry issues and parenting skills often go hand in hand.

My daughter Christy recently interrupted me in the middle of a message to ask, "Can I leave now?" With every parent checking out my parenting skills, I smiled, gave her an empathetic no, and decided I'd better read this book again.

JIM BURNS, PRESIDENT
NATIONAL INSTITUTE OF YOUTH MINISTRY

Introduction

Like many of you reading this book, I was raised within the friendly walls of the local church—destined for Glory from day one! I remember Dad serving as an elder, teaching Sunday School, and singing in the choir. Mom was the choir director. I served as president of the youth group *and* dated the minister's daughter. On the surface I had it made.

But, as is so often the case, looks were deceiving. I was more Christianized than Christian. And to be honest, it took me a while to figure out the difference. In the process, I kept my youth minister, church leaders, and parents all guessing.

One week I was a spiritual dynamo, the next completely apathetic. One month I was excited about service and the next, rebellious to the core. One year I would be motivated to evangelize my friends and the next, turning them off with my own brand of legalistic lip service and fundamentalist fire.

Thank God for His grace! Through the years, my faith has grown and matured as the Holy Spirit has smoothed some of my rough edges. But what goes around, comes around. And now God has called me to work with my own kind: church youth.

Teens who have grown up in the church, although uniquely blessed, also face challenges as they struggle to make their faith their own. For the non-Christian kids who attend your group, the challenge is salvation. For the newly converted, the challenge is basic Christian teaching and discipleship. But for the long-time Christians in your group, the challenges are different. By examining these challenges and other issues, it is my hope that you'll come to a better understanding of what makes these students "tick" and discover how to minister to them more effectively.

Be encouraged. Working with church youth can be a tremendously rewarding ministry. Aiding these students in the process of becoming "complete in Christ" (Colossians 1:28) may take some time. But with patience, love, patience, understanding, patience, encouragement, patience, humor, patience, insight, patience, and *prayer*, you'll begin to see changes in your students' lives. From one who's been there . . . trust me, I know.

YOUTH WHO HAVE GROWN UP IN THE CHURCH

I've always thought "church kids" were, in a way, misunderstood. Let's face it—sometimes they get a bad rap. We've all heard the epithets: "goody-goody," "hypocrite," and the ever-popular "church brat," to name a few. Granted, in certain cases these labels might be justified, but there is much more to church youth than these stereotypes reveal.

Since you're reading this book, you probably have a number of young people in your youth group who have "grown up Christian" and you're searching for ways to better understand them and effectively minister to their special needs. I know it's a concern of mine.

But before we can deal with their struggles or examine any program strategies, we need to look at who these students are. What influences have shaped both who they are in Christ and who they are as individuals? What are the effects of growing up Christian?

Let's take a peek into the lives of these students and the two places that have influenced them the most—their homes and their churches.

BORN BELIEVERS

Biology was always one of my favorite subjects in school. Put me in a class with a couple of squeamish sophomore girls and a sheep's brain, and the terror I could create was amazing! But seriously, I did enjoy the *study* of biology; the characteristics and complexities of life always fascinated me. Today, as a youth pastor, I am still interested in biology. As a matter of fact, did you know that you can use biology to understand the relationships between parents, teens, and the faith? For example, when the principles of reproduction are applied to the Christian family, you come to realize that a vast number of teens have come to the faith as a result of their heritage. In other words, they're born into it.

A great number of churched youth in America have grown up in the faith and are what I would call biological Christians. These teens represent second, third, and even fourth generation believers and likely make up a significant part of your youth group. In a large church where I previously helped minister to over 400 high school students, we found that more than 85% had grown up in the church.

Whatever percentage of your youth group these "bios" make up, I'm sure you've begun to see that they have a special set of characteristics that need to be addressed when ministering to them. But before we proceed to those, let's take a look at the biblical data that teaches the importance of perpetuating the faith through successive generations.

PASSING ON THE FAITH

The practice of passing the faith on from one generation to another began with God's people during the time of Moses. After 40 years of marching in the wilderness, and just prior to entering the Promised Land, Moses instructed the Israelites to raise their children and all following generations in the ways of the Lord:

> Now this is the commandment, the statutes and the judgments which the Lord your God has commanded me to teach you, that you might do them in the land where you are going over to possess it, so that you and your son and your grandson might fear the Lord your God, to keep all His statutes and His commandments, which I command you, all the days of your life, and that your days may be prolonged. And these words, which I am commanding you today, shall be on your heart; and you shall teach them diligently to your sons and shall talk of them when you sit in your house and when you walk by the way and when you lie down and when you rise up.
> (Deuteronomy 6:1-2, 6-7)

This passage reveals the biblical mandate for parents to raise their children in the instruction of the Lord through both teaching and example. It is interesting to note that God's original intent for the practice of what we now call youth ministry was that it be done through the family. Naturally, generations of teens came to the faith by the influence of their parents. But times have changed since the days of Moses. An adolescent subculture, with concerns that Moses' generation couldn't have dreamed of, now exists. However, the principle of parental example and instruction of the faith is still crucial.

Commenting on this theme in his article from the book *Parents and Teenagers*, Dan Sartin added, "There should be something in the lives of parents that compels children to believe. . . . You transfer your faith to your children by your example. You should be sensitive and seek the right to be heard by your children. And you should come from a position of authority that is gained by respect as well as inheritance."[1]

This practice of passing the faith from one generation to another is also evident in the New Testament. When speaking of the family background of his young assistant, Timothy, Paul said, "For I am mindful of the sincere faith within you, which first dwelt in your grandmother Lois, and your mother Eunice, and I am sure that it is in you as well" (2 Timothy 1:5).

Several observations can be made regarding ministry to church youth. First, whether they are considered a blessing or a challenge, it is likely that they will always be represented as a specific subculture within your youth group. They are the product of Christian upbringing, whether it be exemplary or deficient.

Dan Jessen, assistant professor of Christian education at Gordon-Conwell Theological Seminary, commented:

A solid Christian home is the single most important factor in the development of Christian young adults. Teenagers from good Christian homes (and from even not-so-good Christian homes) tend to stay with the faith. Those whose parents are not committed to Christ tend to fall away. Conversely, the bulk of teenagers who are active youth group members but fail to survive usually come from homes where the parents did not model Christian faith.[2]

Second, realize that being raised in a Christian home is a divine privilege that not all Christian teens have been blessed with. And as Jessen mentioned, trying to live as a Christian teen in a non-Christian home can be a struggle at the very least.

Dave, for example, was a great kid who came from a non-Christian background. He began visiting my youth group during his sophomore year in high school and soon became a Christian. On the night of his conversion, Dave excitedly ran home to share the good news with his parents. But, unfortunately, his parents didn't think his news was so good. Instead of receiving their support or even a small measure of approval, Dave got a look of disgust and a warning from his parents to "keep his [newly found] religion to himself." Dave's non-Christian home created for him the kind of struggle that most church youth never have to face.

Although some teens resent certain aspects of their Christian upbringing for one reason or another, the majority I've found are grateful for their "heavenly" heritage; I know because I'm one of them. My Christian roots go back to the mid-19th century with the conversion of my great-grandparents. Their decision to follow Christ has resulted in five generations of Christians in our family, of which I proudly belong to the fourth.

Finally, although these students are blessed by their Christian upbringing, being "born into" the faith also presents certain struggles. We'll be looking at many of these in later chapters.

BORN BELIEVING?

Of course, theologically speaking, being born into a Christian family no more makes one a believer than eating Wheaties makes someone a professional athlete or going to K-mart makes him a blue-light special. No one receives a genetic membership card from God with his picture on it and the caption *Club Heaven* — although I encountered a high school student who sincerely thought he was a Christian because his parents were. He was attempting to "ride" his parents' spiritual coattails all the way to the gates of heaven!

Donald E. Sloat, author of *The Dangers of Growing Up in a Christian Home*, commented on the need for church youth to develop a personalized faith:

> Christian values and knowledge . . . cannot be passed simply from one generation to the next because they have to become personally meaningful in an individual's life and experience. This requires years of living and learning from successes as well as mistakes. Since we all tend to learn the hard way from our own experiences rather than from our parents' experiences, we often repeat the mistakes of prior generations; hence the expression, "History repeats itself."[3]

It's been said that God has no grandchildren, and I think Scripture firmly supports this idea. As Jesus was speaking to the multitudes, He exhorted them to "believe in the light, in order that you may become *sons* of light" (John 12:36, italics added). Jesus used the word *sons* to describe His followers, not grandsons (or for that matter, *daughters*, instead of granddaughters). Therefore, believers have a *direct*, not indirect, relationship with the Lord.

Perhaps John 14:6 is clearest on this point. Jesus said, "I am the way, and the truth, and the life; no one comes to the Father, but through Me," (not through *your parents* and Me).

I think we all understand that no teen will automatically embrace the faith just because he or she has grown up in the church and a Christian home. As a matter of fact, in a 1980 study of people who left the church, David Roozen found that 46% of Americans stopped participating in religious activity at some point in their lives. And he found the age of abandonment was highest among adolescent youth.[4]

Despite this alarming dropout rate among church youth, it should be noted that the majority of those raised in the church *do* remain faithful. I've had the privilege of discipling many young people who have been reared in the faith and who are today models of Christian service and leadership.

COMMON COMPLAINTS AND WARNING SIGNS

As we all know, the teen years are a time of difficult transition. Students are often preoccupied with issues like peer pressure, acceptance, dating relationships, and other concerns that may overshadow their desires for spiritual growth. As a result, students sometimes begin to see their church and their faith a little differently. And when these struggles arise, students may express themselves in the only way many of them can think of—they complain!

Now don't get me wrong, these struggles are normal and healthy in most cases. But to the average youth worker, these comments sometimes can get tiresome and a little frustrating. I'm sure they sound all too familiar:

- "I wish I weren't a Christian so I could go out and have fun like the rest of my friends at school."
- "Youth group is boring. How come we never do anything fun like take trips to Hawaii or go on Caribbean cruises?"

- "The youth pastor thinks *everything* is satanic—I'm sure!"
- "I would never bring my friends to youth group—how embarrassing!"
- "I like going to youth group to see my friends, but that's about it."
- "I don't have time to be involved in youth group because I'm already involved in things at school."
- "Church is nothing but a guilt trip; who needs it?"
- "The youth group is full of hypocrites—I want out!"
- "I'm not challenged personally or spiritually. It's all so shallow."
- "I'm not accepted. Everyone's cliquey."

Do we write off these complaints as petty and insignificant? Maybe we should pay closer attention. According to a recent survey of unchurched adults who left the church in their teenage years, many cite these same complaints as the basis for their abandonment. Here is a sample of responses given[5]:

I got involved in other things:	26%
I was put off by hypocrites:	20%
Church was dull, boring:	17%
It wasn't meeting my needs:	14%
Self-righteous people made me leave:	8%
I began doing things that conflicted with church teachings:	4%

Surveys like this one and others indicate that the complaints we hear now might end up being the reasons some of our young people leave in the future.

In most cases, what these church youth are really saying is, "Listen to us!" However, often we don't. Sometimes rather than attempt to understand the needs and struggles of church youth, we simply throw up our hands and say, "That's just the way they are!" or "It's just a phase they're going through."

In response, I've heard myself spouting a list of my own complaints:

- "They're bored with the Bible. All they want are sex and dating talks and studies on the Book of Revelation!"
- "They only come to youth group for social reasons."

- "They can't get into worship."
- "They want an entertainment ministry with a comedian for a youth minister who feeds them ice cream and pizza, rather than spiritual food."
- "They don't witness. Getting them to share their faith is like pulling teeth from a hungry alligator!"
- "They're selfish and apathetic."
- "They're out to test my authority."
- "They're cliquey and don't accept non-Christian kids easily into the group. As a matter of fact, I don't even think they like non-Christians!"

Do all these complaints have validity? *Yes!* Are solutions easily found? *No.* However, by identifying the struggles and acknowledging their importance, we can begin to address these needs in a meaningful way. But before we try to figure out *why* these students are the way they are and *how* we can best reach them, I'd like to introduce you to a few of my favorite youth group characters!

WHO ARE THESE KIDS?

You've heard it said that "it takes one to know one." Well, being a former youth group "challenge" myself, I'd like to offer a description of some of the more common personality types you might have hanging around your youth group. I'm sure you'll recognize some of them; they're not difficult to spot.

TYPE #1 — THE WALKING CONCORDANCE
This individual knows all about the Bible and will gladly answer any question you've ever had on the subject. Equipped with memory verses and Bible awards dating back to the church nursery, this student prides himself on scriptural knowledge. However, he or she doesn't seem to put much of it into practice.

TYPE #2 — THE ATTITUDINAL APATHETIC
This person has also heard it all before from the crib up. But unlike the Walking Concordance, he would much rather tune out than tune in. He is forced to go to youth meetings by his parents and when in attendance lets everyone know how bored he is with

the entire situation. As one youth worker put it, "This teen is content . . . to sing 'Just as I am' while he remains just as he is."[6]

TYPE #3—MR. REBELLIOUS
This troubled and confused young person feels Christianity has ripped him off of all the "fun" (partying, sex, etc.) he sees his non-Christian friends having. He's made up his mind to rebel at home and school and to cause as much chaos as is humanly possible at youth group meetings. What a guy!

TYPE #4—THE POLITE AND PUNCTUAL PASSIVE OBSERVER
These young people are very, very, very obedient, polite, and nice Christians. They will do or believe almost anything you tell them. Their attendance at youth meetings is impeccable, but their real, meaningful involvement is minimal.

TYPE #5—THE WORKAHOLIC WORRYWART
These teens are usually very sincere, though often confused and troubled. Not only do they view the Christian life as a list of do's and don'ts, but they also see opportunities for Christian service as a means of attaining spiritual brownie points. And when they feel they're not doing enough, they will usually worry to the point of doubting their own salvation.

TYPE #6—I THINK, THEREFORE I DOUBT
Usually in their late teens, these reflective, intelligent young people begin to question the faith that they have taken at face value for so long. Some are sincere and truly interested in finding out the answers, while others simply become skeptical and critical. Both types want their theological questions answered. But more importantly, they want to know that all this "Christianity business" really works in the "real world."

TYPE #7—THE DISCIPLINE PROBLEM LOOKING FOR A PLACE TO HAPPEN
No teen is typical when it comes to discipline, but this student is usually a pretty good kid who just can't sit still for more than five minutes. This particular individual not only has a reputation among the Christian education department for his excess energy, but he knows it and is proud of it. Just try to show him a corner in the church he hasn't spent some significant amount of time in!

Obviously, this is not an exhaustive list, and not all church youth will manifest these characteristics. In fact, many are quite enthusiastic, cooperative, spiritually oriented, and balanced as they strive to grow in their Christian walks. But realize that the subculture of "biologicals" in your group *are* different than other teens who make up your student population. Whether obedient or belligerent, enthusiastic or apathetic, these students share a common Christian upbringing and heritage that affects them all in some way. And as we mentioned earlier, these effects are not to be taken lightly.

Now that we've met some of these kids, let's take a look at factors that contributed to their development as biological Christians. I call them the privileges and pains of growing up Christian.

THE PRIVILEGES OF GROWING UP CHRISTIAN

1. KNOWLEDGE OF GOD'S LOVE AND FORGIVENESS
Christian children come to understand and experience God's love and forgiveness at an early age through the models of their parents and the church. Many people I know who have come to the faith in later life have shared with me that they wish they had known of Christ's love in earlier years. Although forgiven, these individuals often are scarred by the guilt, hurts, and consequences of poor decisions and actions from the past. Ideally, students who've grown up with the knowledge of God's love and forgiveness won't have as many of these problems to deal with.

2. CHRISTIAN MORAL AND ETHICAL STANDARDS
More and more we are seeing the painful and even tragic consequences of conforming to the world's lack of morality. Ideally, students raised in a Christian family have the fiber of godly ethics and values woven into their character from birth. Not only does this heritage help them distinguish right from wrong, but it provides them with a Christian worldview for decision-making. This moral guideline may save students from having to learn life's lessons the "hard way."

3. SUPPORT OF CHRISTIAN FELLOWSHIP AND POSITIVE PEER INFLUENCES
It is no news to youth workers that peer pressure is the most powerful influence on a teenager's life. The opportunity of being

part of a Christian youth group potentially provides a positive peer influence and support group that most teenagers don't have.

4. EXPOSURE TO CHRISTIAN ROLE MODELS

The age when youth could look up to and admire a hero is all but gone. Traditional role models such as professional athletes, celebrities, political leaders, and even those in the ministry have succumbed to the integrity crisis we've all become too familiar with. But like you, I know many in the church who still practice what they preach and have a heart for ministering to children and teens. These men and women of character provide lifetime examples for them to follow, a benefit few non-Christian young people have.

5. KNOWLEDGE AND APPLICATION OF SCRIPTURE

Being exposed to God's Word at an early age provides teens with a working knowledge of the ultimate truth from which they can discern the world's philosophies and teachings.

6. BEGINNING THE PROCESS OF CHRISTIAN GROWTH AND MATURITY

Christian discipleship begins early when children learn about God in the church and the home. These youth are often more stable and mature in their Christian walks than some of the more enthusiastic new Christians because they have had time to live with their faith and put it to the test. Although we are often frustrated with their status quo Christianity, they are also not as subject to the radical "falls" that often plague the teenage convert.

7. HOPE

In a 1987 survey *USA Today* conducted on the topic of teenage worries, the majority of teens surveyed worried most about the death of a parent, car accident, plane crash, being abducted by a stranger, nuclear war, and dying.[7] Christian youth are concerned about these same issues, but they have the assurance of their ultimate salvation and eternal destiny with the Lord.

THE PAINS OF GROWING UP CHRISTIAN

1. A LEGALISTIC HOME

I've encountered many well-meaning Christian couples who have attempted to raise their children with a firm hand, not sparing the rod to spoil the child (Proverbs 13:24). However, in their desire to raise disciplined and obedient children, many parents unknowingly create a legalistic and authoritarian home environment. At its worst, parental obedience becomes forced obligation and the Christian life, a standard of do's and don'ts instead of a relationship. When children from these families reach their teenage years, too often rebellion is the unfortunate response.

2. GUILT FROM NOT MEASURING UP TO HIGH EXPECTATIONS
Moral failure, lukewarmness, and spiritual complacency are key factors in the disillusionment of church youth. Depression and guilt may result as teens struggle with living the sanctified life.

3. LACK OF IMPRESSIVE TESTIMONY
As a high schooler, I can remember many times hearing the "black and white" testimony of some ex-drug addict, Christian rock star. How God had obviously worked in that person's life seemed so great. I often wished that I had had a conversion experience like that. Instead, mine was more gray than black and white. I just kind of flowed into the faith. Many church youth, like me, do not have an impressive conversion experience and, at times, feel like second-class Christians. Not only can insecurities and unwarranted doubts arise, but a lack of evangelistic fervor may also result.

4. BOREDOM WITH CHURCH AND THE CHRISTIAN LIFE
Webster defines boredom as a condition of being "tediously devoid of interest." After years of hearing the same old Bible stories, singing the same old songs, and playing the same old games, teens may understandably become uninterested in what the church offers them. When a youth ministry perpetuates the same old things, no one should be surprised if rigor mortis sets in! The result is a group of apathetic students who, although they appear bored on the outside, are begging on the inside for opportunities to get involved.

5. STRUGGLES TO OWN THEIR FAITH
The junior and senior years of high school are often characterized by a teen's struggle to own his or her own faith. Students face the reality that they have been holding their parents' "spiritual" hands and really haven't made conscious decisions to follow the Lord for

themselves. They may wrestle with their beliefs, church doctrine, and relationship with their Christian parents. Out of this critical struggle will emerge the foundations of adult faith or potential abandonment.

6. CURIOSITY WITH SIN

Although being raised with Christian morality is overwhelmingly positive, the sometimes sheltered (or in some cases, semi-victorian) life of a Christian teen can also have a backlash. Like me, you've probably had a student say to you, "I'd like to [insert sin] just once. I just want to see what it's like."

Regardless of their upbringing, Christian students often have natural curiosities about the "pleasures of sin." Dr. Robert Laurent has observed, "Because teenagers spend so much time outside the home with their friends, it is understandable that peers often have a greater influence on adolescent attitudes, speech, appearance, and behavior than the family has. If members of the peer group experiment with [sex], tobacco, alcohol, and drugs, teenagers are 'likely to do the same.' "[8]

What a list of issues! With so many factors to consider, it's like trying to piece together a spiritual jigsaw puzzle for every teen in your group! Perhaps some of you are even wondering if you have all the pieces. (Puzzles can be so complex!)

Relax. Two of the major pieces are about to be fitted into place as we take a look at the roles of the Christian home and church in the overall picture of understanding church youth.

THINK ABOUT IT

1. What percentage of the students in your group are "biological" Christians?

2. Reflect on your own Christian background. How many generations back (if any) does the faith go in your family?

3. How might your Christian background affect the way you relate to and work with the students—both those from Christian and those from unbelieving homes—in your group?

4. How do you usually respond to the Attitudinal Apathetic students in your group?

NOTES

1. Don Sartin, "Is Your Faith Rubbing Off on Your Kids?" in *Parents & Teenagers*, ed. Jay Kesler, with Ronald A. Beers (Wheaton, Illinois: Victor Books, 1984), p. 336.
2. Dan Jessen, "United We Stand—Developing Your Parent-Youth Worker Alliance," *Youthworker Journal 4* (Winter 1987): 35.
3. Donald E. Sloat, *The Dangers of Growing Up in a Christian Home* (Nashville, Tennessee: Thomas Nelson Publishers, 1986), pp. 26–27.
4. David A. Roozen, "Church Dropouts: Changing Patterns of Disengagement and Re-entry," *Review of Religious Research* v. 21 (Fall 1990): 427.
5. Doug Self, "Who Are the Unchurched?" in *The Youth Ministry Resource Book*, ed. Eugene C. Roehlkepartain (Loveland, Colorado: Group Books, 1988), p. 70.
6. Dr. Robert Laurent, *Keeping Your Teen in Touch with God* (Elgin, Illinois: David C. Cook Publishing Co., 1988), p. 17.
7. Karen Peterson, "Young Minds Can Carry a Heavy Load of Worries," *USA Today*, 26 May 1987, p. 6D.
8. Laurent, p. 95.

CHAPTER TWO

THE CHRISTIAN HOME

During a recent talk on parents, I asked my high school students, Is your family more like . . .

(a) the Adams family,
(b) the Brady bunch,
(c) the Cosby family, or
(d) the Manson family?

With options like these, I knew the responses were sure to be varied. Family situations from basically normal (if you can call the Cosby family normal; they're closer to unbelievable!) to weird, strange, and even deranged were given. Unfortunately, some students also described their families in more painful ways using adjectives such as "broken," "neglected," and "unbearable." And remember, we're talking about Christian families!

Whatever happened to the "typical" Christian family where Dad is the spiritual leader, Mom the supportive and capable wife, and the kids emotionally well-balanced and obedient?

Answer: The Christian family has, in many ways, fallen victim to the same pressures and misfortunes as the secular family. In his popular book *Megatrends*, John Naisbitt analyzed the modern American family in this fashion:

> Most of us . . . were raised in a typical nuclear American family: Father was breadwinner, mother took care of house and children, usually two. But today, there is no such thing as a typical family. And only a distinct minority (7 percent) of America's population fits the traditional family profile. . . .
>
> Today's family can be a single parent (male or female) with one or more children, a two-career couple with no children, a female breadwinner with child and househusband, or a blended family that consists of a previously married couple and a combination of children from those two previous marriages.[1]

As you well know, the Christian community has not been immune to the changes that have taken place within the family during the past several decades. Regretfully, it is often the children who pay the price for this loss of stability in the home. When the natural environment of the family is disrupted by divorce or other circumstances, a child loses his or her sense of security, which can result in a number of problems. Many of these emerge in the form of behavioral difficulty and emotional imbalances, particularly evident during the teen years.

Often, whether the family is traditional or nontraditional, parents turn to the youth worker for help and guidance, sometimes even expecting a "quick fix" in hopes of straightening out their troubled teen. What many of these concerned parents fail to realize is the lasting impact that the previous years of parental and family influence have made on their child.

CHECKING UNDER THE HOOD

During college, a friend of mine had her car stolen so she was in the market for a new one. Her previous mode of transportation, although not flashy, was practical and reliable. All she had to do was turn the ignition and the car faithfully would start up. The only maintenance necessary was to keep "old faithful" gassed up and check the oil once in awhile.

But my friend wasn't in the market for a practical car this time around. She wanted something that would turn heads! Before I knew it, she had her heart set on a sporty, little European car—a cherry red convertible. And yes, she *would* look good in it! But despite my efforts to warn her about the unreliability of such cars and the expense (not to mention frequency!) of maintenance, my words of caution fell on deaf ears. And to make matters worse, she bought the car without first taking it to a mechanic to check under the hood. It looked fine on the outside, seemed to run all right, and that was all that really mattered to her. Unfortunately, my friend learned that appearances can be deceiving—she had bought herself a sporty, cherry red, convertible LEMON!

In working with Christian families for more than a decade, I've found that it pays to check under the family "hood" of every teen you're dealing with. The more you understand about the home, the better you will be able to deal with a student's particular behavior and problems. In working with youth, appearances can be very, very deceiving indeed.

In my first youth ministry, I had a freckle-faced, puppy-eyed, little, tag-along freshman named Brian. This likable young man was new to the youth group and before too long had most of my adult volunteer staff (myself included) wrapped around his little finger. It seemed everything he did was so cute and boyish; we just gave in to his every request for time and attention—sometimes to the neglect of some of the other students.

What it took us rookie youth workers awhile to figure out was that Brian's need for attention and his subtly manipulative ways of getting it were a direct result of a disrupted family situation. In other words, he had a problem under the hood.

Once we checked it out, we found that Brian had been struggling with the consequences of a divorce that had left him insecure and starving for attention and love. By checking under the hood and finding out more about his home life, my staff and I were then able to minister to Brian more effectively by responding to his real need for attention and acceptance in more appropriate and helpful ways.

Not only is it important for the youth worker to know if a particular student comes from a traditional or nontraditional family makeup, but it is also crucial to be aware of the style of parenting and Christian modeling that has gone on in the home. By examining these areas, the youth worker will be better equipped to deal with an abundance of ministry opportunities that will present themselves during a young person's teen years.

TEACHINGS IN THE CHRISTIAN HOME

One of the primary mandates of a Christian home is that it provide an environment for raising children "in the discipline and instruction of the Lord" (Ephesians 6:4). Most Christian parents realize their responsibilities of teaching and raising their children in the faith.

The Bible is filled with practical advice and admonitions for rearing children in accordance with God's will. However, there are several general areas worth mentioning. These are the most common teachings in Christian homes.

1. LOVE FOR GOD AND NEIGHBOR
"You shall love the Lord your God with all your heart, and with all your soul, and with all your mind." This is the great and foremost commandment. The second is like it, "You shall love your neighbor as yourself." (Matthew 22:37-39)

2. THE IMPORTANCE OF GOING TO CHURCH
And let us consider how to stimulate one another to love and good deeds, not forsaking our own assembling together, as is the habit of some. (Hebrews 10:24-25)

And they were continually devoting themselves to the apostles' teaching and to fellowship, to the breaking of bread and to prayer. (Acts 2:42)

3. ACCEPTANCE OF SCRIPTURE AND DAILY BIBLE READING
All Scripture is inspired by God and profitable for teaching, for reproof, for correction, for training in righteousness; that the man of God may be adequate, equipped for every good work.
(2 Timothy 3:16-17)

4. PERSONAL PRAYER LIFE

But you, when you pray, go into your inner room, and when you have shut your door, pray to your Father who is in secret, and your Father who sees in secret will repay you.   (Matthew 6:6)

5. MORAL BEHAVIOR

Flee immorality. Every other sin that a man commits is outside the body, but the immoral man sins against his own body. Or do you not know that your body is a temple of the Holy Spirit who is in you, whom you have from God, and that you are not your own? For you have been bought with a price: therefore glorify God in your body.   (1 Corinthians 6:18-20)

6. OBEDIENCE TO PARENTS

Children, obey your parents in the Lord, for this is right. Honor your father and mother (which is the first commandment with a promise), that it may be well with you, and that you may live long on the earth.   (Ephesians 6:1-3)

Depending on a family's particular denomination or practice, certain additional areas of spiritual emphasis may be taught. For example, Pentecostal families might stress the importance of discovering spiritual gifts, while Lutheran or Catholic homes may emphasize the importance of catechetical studies. Of course there will be many issues in one home that are hardly mentioned in another. But in any case, the student coming from a Christian home has the potential of being raised in an environment where a knowledge of God and the Christian life are foundational for personal growth, development, and maturity.

Yet, perhaps the most important thing a youth worker can know about a student's home environment is not *what* was taught or said but *how* it was communicated.

STYLES OF PARENTING

Traditionally, experts on the family recognize three parenting styles. These styles can communicate as much to the young person as the words themselves. One is the permissive style of parenting, which says, "OK, go ahead and do it your own way if you want to." Another is the authoritarian approach, which says,

26

"You'll do it, and you'll do it now because I said so!"

The third is the authoritative style, which says, "I can understand why you want to do it that way, but here's some information about how to do it correctly. Let's try it this way." Of course, the authoritative style of parenting is the most balanced approach, combining fairness with firmness. But unfortunately, recognizing which is the best model and being able to practice it can be two completely different things.

MODEL OF PARENTING STYLES

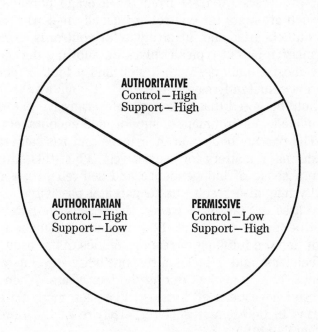

Support = The ability to make the child feel loved and accepted.
Control = The ability of parents to manage a child's behavior.

For this reason, it is important that you try to understand and recognize each parenting style so as to minister more effectively to the students in your group.

STYLE #1—PERMISSIVE
There will undoubtedly be a number of students in your group who come from homes where a permissive style of parenting oper-

ates. Webster defines the word permissive as "allowing freedom . . . tolerant, indulgent." With this in mind, let's take a look at the permissive home environment.

Permissive parents typically do not control their child's behavior with a military-like fashion of discipline. They do not feel comfortable barking out orders with the threat of harsh punishment if their demands are not met. Instead, the permissive approach attempts to appeal to the teen's sense of reason and uses logical argumentation when trying to persuade. Unfortunately, since many teens are neither reasonable nor logical in many of their thought processes (at least from the average parent's point of view), such attempts for control are usually met with resistance. When conflicts arise and the struggle for control is at its fiercest, the permissive parent typically gives in, allowing the teen to manipulate most situations. With a sigh and a look of displeasure, this parent reluctantly says, "OK, have it your way then."

It should be noted that a strength of permissive parents is that they provide an environment of support and encouragement in the home. The parents believe in their teens and basically trust them to decide many matters for themselves. While this situation can produce a sense of independence and self-reliance, a feeling of insecurity may also result due to parental passivity.

In the area of control, however, the permissive parent is weak and can be lenient to a fault. Few demands are made for proper behavior and the fulfilling of responsibilities. As a result, inappropriate behavior and a lack of responsibility develop within the child, most clearly evident during the teen years. When authority and control have been all but lost, I've seen many parents raise their arms in defeat and declare, "They're in the Lord's hands now. There's nothing I can do."

In tears I have prayed with Christian parents who have witnessed their children, uncontrolled and troubled, drift further and further away from them and the Lord. In hindsight, they remember the words of Solomon, "He who spares his rod hates his son, but he who loves him disciplines him diligently" (Proverbs 13:24).

STYLE #2 — AUTHORITARIAN

Dr. Diana Baumrind, a noted researcher on the subject of parenting styles, identifies the authoritarian parent as one who "values obedience as a virtue and favors punitive, forceful measures to curb self-will at points where the child's actions or beliefs conflict with what [the parent] think is right or correct."² The authoritarian parent is typically characterized by rules without relationship and law without love. An environment is created in the home that is oftentimes rigid and inflexible. An atmosphere of law, rather than grace, tends to abound.

Young people coming from authoritarian homes know that Mom and Dad mean business when a command is not obeyed. Spankings (when they were younger), groundings, and loss of privileges are all familiar territory to these students. Issues of contention are not diplomatically discussed or compromised. "I'm the parent, and you'll do as I say" is the standard response to the questioning adolescent.

Although it may sometimes seem that these parents do not have their children's best interests at heart, as with the permissive style, these parents are simply trying to do what they think is best for their children. Unfortunately, their style of correction often fuels the fire of their children's resistance as tensions continue to build. Colossians 3:21 admonishes, "Fathers, do not exasperate your children, that they may not lose heart." The Greek word for exasperate can also be translated "provoke," as in the *New King James Version*, and carries with it the idea of purposeful intent.

I am reminded of a television special I saw on the story of the singing group The Beach Boys. The show portrayed the father of three of the boys in the group as an overbearing, verbally abusive "drill sergeant" who purposefully exasperated and provoked his sons to perform to his high expectations. His authoritarian manner led to discouragement and even emotional damage in the lives of several of his sons. Eventually, the boys had to fire their father as manager of the band just so they could carry on, before they completely lost heart.

There may be teens in your group who have lost motivation and are discouraged because of an overly strict, authoritarian home environment. Merton and Irene Strommen, in a study of 7,050 high school youth, found that 39% of those surveyed felt "bothered either 'very much,' or 'quite a bit' by the fact that 'My parents are too strict.' " They explained,

In that study we found that one result of extreme strictness was greater tension in the home. In comparisons between groups, we found greater family disunity and more distance between parents and youth in the families of overly strict parents than any other group. We found the effect of over-control on youth to be lower self-esteem and heightened feelings of self-condemnation. Another frequent outcome is parent-youth conflict, with life in the home becoming an ongoing power struggle.[3]

The Strommens went on to conclude,

> Adolescents raised under autocratic [authoritarian] control are more likely to be characterized by the following behaviors: hostility to parents; age prejudice; antisocial activities (for example, stealing, lying, fighting, vandalism); feelings of social alienation; rejection of traditional moral standards; and inability to relate well to people. An overly strict approach also encourages a more prejudicial and judgmental spirit in the adolescent.[4]

Indeed, such outcomes represent the negative effects of the authoritarian style of parenting where control is high but expressed love, support, and encouragement are minimal.

STYLE #3—AUTHORITATIVE

While firmness and freedom characterize the authoritarian and permissive styles of parenting, respectively, the authoritative approach seeks to present a model of balance between the two. The majority of Christian parents I know strive for a fair but firm authoritative and democratic approach. However, most parents at least occasionally slide into a pattern of inconsistency between the two extremes. On the one hand, parents don't want to be walked on by their kids; but on the other, they want a healthy relationship with them. It's a difficult line to maintain.

In one circumstance parents might use an authoritarian tone with their teens: "You took the car without asking. You're grounded for two weeks, and that's final!" In another situation, they might respond more permissively: "I'm tired of your whining (sigh); go ahead and color your hair orange. I don't care."

Youth workers must realize that parenting is perhaps the most difficult assignment on earth (with the possible exception of surviving a junior high all-nighter). It's tough to be both fair and firm in every circumstance. But Paul's words support the authoritative and balanced approach to Christian parenting that should be the aim in every home: "Fathers, do not provoke your children to anger; but bring them up in the discipline and instruction of the Lord" (Ephesians 6:4).

The authoritative style of parenting is characterized by a supportive, encouraging, and loving manner in raising a child according to the teachings of Scripture. At the same time, parents recognize that teens are younger, less mature, and less knowledgeable in many areas of life. At times, they will require parental discipline with a firm hand and steady confidence.

Finally, an authoritative style of parenting is characterized by an attitude of self-control on the part of the parents. As author Fritz Ridenour has noted, "The authoritative parent uses *self-control*, not to manipulate or dominate, but to nurture and train."[5]

Unfortunately, the attempted use of self-control by the well-meaning parent is constantly challenged (in most cases) by the average, self-respecting teen trying to flex his or her muscles toward independence. Areas of contention classically include choice of friends, dating relationships, responsibilities at home, transportation, and school. In many cases, the parents' use of self-control is tested beyond measure, and the temptation to use an authoritarian ("I'm not going to take this anymore!") or permissive ("Fine, you win. Go ahead.") approach seems the natural response. Again, I like Ridenour's encouragement to parents in his book on parent-teen relationships. "To parent authoritatively you are to nurture as you negotiate, but not drive your teenager to discouragement, or worse."[6]

Remember, these broad categories are not designed to overgeneralize. Rather, they provide guidelines for understanding in order to help youth workers better assess student home environments and, in turn, better minister to their students.

Now that we've had a chance to examine the dynamics of several parenting styles, let's continue to "check under the hood" of the Christian family in terms of what's been modeled. For as the familiar saying goes, "More is caught than taught."

MODELING IN THE CHRISTIAN HOME

Parental instruction can only be as strong as parental modeling. When I was a teenager, I listened to and acted upon the instructions of my father because he backed them up with his actions.

Dad was a man of morality, integrity, and honesty. When he taught us kids that drunkenness and swearing were not compatible with our Christian faith we heard the message loud and clear. Not so much because he said it, but because Dad didn't use foul language (even when he was real mad) nor did he drink. I cannot remember a time when I saw a can of beer or a bottle of wine in our refrigerator. My father's words were consistent with his actions. He lived his Christianity not only at church, but at home too. I thank God for his model. It's made a lasting impact on my faith.

Jay Kesler also expressed the importance of being a consistent model as a parent. "No amount of money spent on teens, no amount of effort spent trying to identify with their fashions, fads, and interests, will take the place of parents who live consistent lives before God and before their children."[7]

Unfortunately, not all Christian parents communicate a consistent Christian lifestyle. Instead, they sometimes preach an empty and hypocritical message of "do as I say, not as I do." For example, most parents deplore the thought of their teens reading pornographic magazines, but many think nothing of bringing home movies that depict extramarital affairs and sex outside of marriage.

The message caught by the confused teen is: My parents are complete hypocrites, saying one thing and doing another. As a youth worker, I've battled this inconsistency game for years with students. It's tough to teach the sanctity of marriage to a young person coming from a broken home or honesty to a student whose father cheats on his taxes, not to mention trying to encourage teens to participate in church services when their parents frequently miss. Unfortunately, improper Christian modeling is not without its consequences.

RESULTS OF INCONSISTENT MODELING

An old adage says, "Your actions speak so loudly I can't hear what you're saying." When a parent's inconsistent actions speak loudly enough, a disillusioned teen may eventually stop listening to anything the parent has to say (especially in religious matters).

Scott was a sophomore in high school and the son of a deacon in our church. His dad stressed the importance of spending personal time in prayer and Bible study, but Scott told me he never saw his father model these disciplines at home. Scott's conclusion about the real importance of his father's faith was that it was fake. As a result, Scott stopped listening to his father's "religious" admonitions.

A second consequence of inconsistent Christian modeling in the home is that teens may begin to imitate, whether directly or indirectly, the behavior they see in their parents. For example, if a parent teaches love and acceptance but constantly employs the use of put-downs and criticism when dealing with his teen, he sows the seeds of a poor self-image. Furthermore, the critical behavior can, and often does, manifest itself in the life of the young person.

Students from verbally abusive homes are often known for exhibiting that same abusiveness among their immediate peer group. The same principle of imitation goes for other areas of behavior. Again, Kesler has observed, "It's absolutely impossible to make an argument against marijuana stick with a kid if you drink alcohol. When fifty thousand people die each year on the highways in alcohol-related accidents, you cannot drink and tell your kids that they shouldn't smoke pot. It won't work. They see the inconsistency."[8]

A final consequence results when the effects of an inconsistent example at home filter into the youth group setting. Teens who have stopped listening to their parents' spiritual instruction may not listen to yours either. In addition, inappropriate and even rebellious behavior can manifest itself openly during youth meetings and activities. And although the student is responsible for his or her own actions, often he or she is simply imitating what is seen at home.

Time for a reality check. The Christian family version of the Cosbys doesn't exist. There are no ideal Christian homes or perfect Christian parents who teach and model consistency 100 percent of the time. (Yes, even dear old Dad fell short occasionally; just ask Mom!)

You can't give your students perfect family situations. The most important things for you to do as a youth worker are to encourage the families you deal with to strive for consistency and to be a support both to parents and students as they face their daily challenges in the home.

STRATEGIES FOR UNDERSTANDING AND MINISTERING TO THE CHRISTIAN FAMILY

As I mentioned earlier, families are a lot like cars. Some run smoothly while others leak oil or stall. As a youth worker, think of yourself as a patient auto mechanic—inspecting, asking questions, and observing a student's family situation carefully before attempting any engine work.

As was mentioned earlier, first make it a point to "check under the hood" of the Christian family. Don't be naïve in thinking that all your students come from well-adjusted families simply because they are Christians. Christian homes can be just as diverse and problem-ridden as non-Christian homes.

Notice first if a young person's family is traditional or nontraditional. Ask yourself questions like these: What are the working situations of the parents? Who are the siblings and what are their relationships? What unique challenges does this family face? Don't be afraid to ask your students these questions. The information will aid you immensely in better understanding what makes them "tick."

Second, visit the families of your students and let them know that you are available and willing to help. But remember, the youth worker's role is to support the ministry already going on in the Christian home. Sometimes well-intentioned youth workers cross the line of support and invade a family's privacy. Your job is not to fix families but to assess the family situation in order to effectively minister to the student. Try not to interfere with a family unless they ask for help or the seriousness of a situation merits it. Your good intentions could be resented. As Anthony Campolo pointed out, "Americans believe not only in separation of church and state but also in separation of church and house."[9]

Third, attempt to determine the parenting styles used in a student's home and adapt your methods of instruction, discipline, and ministry accordingly. For example, I once had a student whose mother was a well-intentioned, authoritarian parent. Her dominant personality exhibited itself in the overprotective and controlling manner in which she dealt with her teenage son.

Maybe this mother had to be that way with Jeff because he was a tough kid and a discipline problem. But every time I slipped and found myself using an authoritarian approach with Jeff (which unfortunately seemed to be my natural response with him), I got the same insolent response he gave his mother. Finally, I started using a more authoritative approach when I addressed, counseled, and disciplined him. I found him to be responsive to this style of communication which seemed to balance what he was used to getting at home. Remember, however, that each teen is different and may or may not respond favorably to the type of parenting employed at home. But an authoritative approach is always a good choice.

Fourth, be aware of the kind of Christian modeling the student is getting at home. While many have the Scriptures both taught and modeled by their parents, others might be confused and struggling with inconsistency. The best way I know to encourage students in their Christian lives is to live your faith confidently before them. If you blow it, admit your weaknesses and be transparent with them. Teenagers respect honesty and integrity.

Finally, provide parents with practical resources and services to aid and encourage them in raising their teens. Parent forums, accountability and support groups, film series, guest speakers, parent newsletters, and activities involving the whole family are all ways a youth worker can help minister to the Christian home.

Most importantly, be open, honest, and available to the parents of your students. You'll find that many are looking for help in raising their teens and that your observations, advice, and support will be more than welcome.

THINK ABOUT IT

1. How do you view the Christian home? Generally, what are your perceptions? Circle the closest response.

    (a) Idealistic   (b) Realistic   (c) Pessimistic

2. On a scale of 1–10, how knowledgeable are you with the family situations of your students?

1	2	3	4	5	6	7	8	9	10
	I don't know much about them			I'm familiar with a few families			I'm familiar with most of them		

3. Think about the various styles of parenting discussed in this

chapter. What style (authoritarian, permissive, authoritative) do you tend to use in dealing with students?

4. Recall the importance of parents modeling the Christian faith in word and in deed. Read Titus 2:11-14, and reflect upon your own example with your students.

5. List several strategies you can begin offering parents that will support, encourage, and strengthen the ministry with their teens that is already going on in the home and will enhance their relationship with you.

6. Pray that God will give you wisdom and discernment in your dealings with the families of your students.

NOTES

1. John Naisbitt, *Megatrends* (New York: Warner Books, 1984), p. 261.
2. Diana Baumrind, "Authoritarian vs. Authoritative Parental Control," *Adolescence* 3 (Fall 1968): 261.
3. Merton P. Strommen and A. Irene Strommen, *Five Cries of Parents* (San Francisco: Harper & Row Publishers, 1985), p. 88.
4. Ibid., pp. 88–89.
5. Fritz Ridenour, *What Teenagers Wish Their Parents Knew about Kids* (Waco, Texas: Word Books, 1982), p. 142.
6. Ibid., p. 143.
7. Jay Kesler, *Ten Mistakes Parents Make with Teenagers* (Brentwood, Tennessee: Wolgemuth & Hyatt, Publishers, Inc., 1988), p. 27.
8. Ibid., p. 26.
9. Anthony Campolo, *Growing Up in America* (Grand Rapids, Michigan: Zondervan Publishing House, 1989), p. 137.

THE CHURCH

Cyndi was an exemplary student as she worked her way through our church's Sunday School department and midweek children's program. Her behavior was always excellent and her knowledge of the Bible quite good. Not only did she have the books of the Bible memorized in order, but she could quote 20 or 30 verses of Scripture she'd learned over the years.

Cyndi sang songs about Jesus with enthusiasm and spirit and was even elected president of the children's choir. Needless to say, I couldn't wait to get her into my youth program.

Unfortunately, the expectations I had for Cyndi were in vain. Something strange happened to Cyndi's spiritual interest and enthusiasm about the time she turned 13. Gone was the pleasant young girl we'd known—she'd become a junior high worker's nightmare!

Entering puberty is one thing, but complete apathy about church and disinterest with the Bible were problems that I had simply not expected with Cyndi. She was indifferent to her youth leaders and became a discipline problem as well. I found myself looking suspiciously at other kids, wondering when they would explode. Where did we (the church, myself) go wrong? Was it the program? Their families? A high-sugar diet?

Many youth workers struggle with situations similar to this one when ministering to church youth. After 11 or 12 years of Christian education, youth workers are expected to continue and even advance the spiritual growth of the young believer. But teenage Christians aren't always cooperative!

Not only can ministry to this special group of adolescents be an awesome challenge, it can get downright frustrating. Youth workers may ask: "Why do they act the way they do? Didn't they learn how to behave in church services in Sunday School?" "They're not motivated to learn a thing about the Bible; do they think they know it all or something? Why do I have such a hard time getting these kids interested in the program?" Before pulling your hair out, remember: Adolescence is the most difficult time of change and transition a person will go through. Young people aren't just changing physically but also intellectually, emotionally, socially, and spiritually.

The task of effectively ministering to church youth during this time is a challenging exercise to say the least. They already know the "ropes" of *churchianity*. That's why it is necessary for the church youth worker to consider the process of adolescent faith development in order to challenge and minister to these students in their *Christianity*.

FAITH DEVELOPMENT

The goal of youth ministry is to evangelize and disciple teens. Colossians 1:28 presents our mission in this way: "And we proclaim Him, admonishing every man and teaching every man with all wisdom, that we may present every man complete in Christ."

Presenting every *teen* complete in Christ is not something that happens automatically once a young Christian graduates into the youth group. A growing faith takes time to mature and develop. Therefore, it is crucial to be aware of the early stages of faith development in order to help a student's faith continue to grow during the adolescent years.

One systematic theologian defined Christian faith as "a certain conviction, wrought in the heart by the Holy Spirit, as to the truth of the Gospel, and a hearty reliance (trust) on the promises of God in Christ."[1] In its practical sense, faith can be understood as an activity of the mind, will, and emotion that responds to the working of the Holy Spirit in the believer's life.

Theorists such as James Fowler (*Stages of Faith*), John Westerhoff III (*Will Our Children Have Faith?*), and Bruce P. Powers (*Growing Faith*), have suggested in their writings helpful insights into the various stages of faith development. V. Bailey Gillespie's book *The Experience of Faith* provides a model of how certain developmental situations in life determine the experiences of faith. Gillespie's categories cover the entire spectrum of faith experience from birth to death, but for our purposes we will explore only those up to and including adolescence.[2]

SITUATIONS OF FAITH EXPERIENCE

Situation One: Borrowed Faith
(Early Childhood, 0–6 Years)

Faith begins in the home. By watching their parents and other family members, children begin to understand the practice, but not necessarily the specific concepts, of their faith. By observing the qualities of trustworthiness, care, support, reliability, and love in parents and even Sunday School teachers, children learn what God is like.

Situation Two: Reflected Faith
(Middle Childhood, 7–12 Years)

During this period, children begin to respond personally to the faith of their parents. The child realizes he or she belongs to the church body. Sunday School teachers become significant to faith development during this time. Feelings of acceptance and belonging within the church basically defines their religious experience especially as children reflect back qualities of openness and trust others. Additional characteristics include: trusting belief, imaginative concept of spiritual things, an interest in the "heroes" of the faith such as Joseph, Moses, and John the Baptist as introduced through story.

Finally, the period of reflected faith is a time when children are most faithful in attendance, as well as the most interested.

Situation Three: Personalized Faith
(Early Adolescence, 13–16 Years)
During these years, youth begin to develop a sense of self-identity. Along with this, they will begin to "own" their faith. Young teens will reflect, evaluate and possibly even reject aspects of their faith as they begin to experience it in more meaningful ways. It is important during this period to put "faith into action." Contradictions and hypocrisy can confuse and discourage young teens. It is also important for the students to be recognized and involved in the church and youth group to maintain their sense of belonging. By the end of this stage, youth will also question and doubt.

Situation Four: Established Faith
(Later Adolescence, 16–18 Years)
For some Christian youth, this period is a time of intense spiritual commitment combined with a desire for putting faith into practice. For others, it's a time of relearning, reorganizing, and reevaluating their prior Christian experience. These youth must thoroughly examine their faith if they are to have complete ownership of it. On the other hand, some will abandon their faith altogether during this time—rejecting its values, beliefs, and practices. Apathy and discouragement can result as teens view the shortcomings of those more mature in the faith. However, as teens begin to own their faith, they will grow in their knowledge, expression and application of it, and their personal relationship with God.

Given the reality of faith development, it's clear that no student is instantly spiritual just because he or she has grown up in the church. The process of Christian growth and maturity takes time. The biological, social, emotional, and intellectual developmental changes these students are going through also greatly affect their experience of faith. With all this in mind, let's examine the role of the church in the development of Christian teens.

IDENTIFYING THE ISSUES

When working with teens who have grown up in the church, you will face different issues than those raised by teens from non-Christian backgrounds. As was briefly mentioned in chapter 1, these students carry an assortment of church "baggage"—most of it beneficial, but some of it a real challenge for you as a youth worker.

1. MOTIVATION

Traditionally, human beings are motivated in two ways: extrinsically and intrinsically. Extrinsic, or external, motivation occurs when an outside force causes us to take action. Rewards, privileges, or punishment are forms of extrinsic motivation. Intrinsic, or internal, motivation comes from a desire within the individual, free from the influence of outside forces, to act on one's own will.

Consider what may have motivated your students as they came up through the ranks of your church's children's program. Typically, Christian education up through elementary school and even junior high uses external motivation. Sunday School teachers often provide buttons, stickers, candy, toys, parties, and even trips to amusement parks to students who succeed in the program. Often children are scored on regular attendance, bringing a Bible and friends, doing their lessons, and learning memory verses.

External motivation for church involvement often continues into the adolescent years too. A high-powered competitive program is sure to attract the young teens in your church, just as free pizza feeds and coed socials will keep high schoolers interested.

To be sure, there is a place for extrinsic motivation in the church. Naturally such methods work well with younger children in helping them learn about the church and Christianity, and extrinsic means of motivation can be great catalysts for outreach among teenagers. However, as youth workers, we need to guard against the mentality of maintaining our students' interests with an endless string of excitement, fun, and games. Let's use extrinsic motivation when and where it is appropriate. But ultimately, for an adolescent's faith to grow and mature, the desire to obey and serve God is going to have to come from within the individual. Youth workers who understand this important concept will provide their students experiences and opportunities that internalize faith.

Leaders who rely on the fun and games approach will ultimately remain frustrated. Even if a youth group "hype" program gets better and better, it will never keep up with the movies, music, parties, and other entertainment that the world is offering teenagers. Offer them the everlasting Word of God and authentic Christianity, and they won't just grab it; they'll hold onto it.

2. OVERFAMILIARITY

For the new Christian entering your junior high program, everything is new and exciting! From salvation, forgiveness of sin, and acceptance, to all-nighters and summer camp—these all bring an enthusiastic response.

Unfortunately, this is not always the case with the seasoned Christian young person. By the end of sixth grade, most kids have worked their way through a good portion of the Old and New Testaments via the Sunday School and midweek children's program. They have learned what it means to be a Christian and how they should treat their neighbors. Many of them have also learned the importance of reaching out to their unsaved friends and regularly bring them to church services and appropriate activities. They have listened to countless sermons and attended enumerable Bible studies, seminars, and retreats. To say these students are familiar with Christianity is certainly an understatement!

For most Christian youth, the process of growth and involvement continues until they are finally mainstreamed into adult congregational life; but for others, the road is a bit more bumpy. When these students get to junior high and high school, you'll find that they simply will not tolerate the same old lessons on the same old biblical content packaged in the same old brown paper wrapper!

Remember the old saying, "Familiarity breeds contempt"? My friend, this same familiarity—yea, *over*familiarity with the Bible and church life in general can breed not only contempt but boredom, apathy, and negative attitudes.

The day when kids will patiently endure a lesson or talk they've heard 20 times before (and I'm serious; they've heard the same messages in Sunday School, church services, camps, conferences, from special speakers, etc.) is long since gone—even if you're a great communicator. Therefore, creative teaching methods and programming are a *must* if church youth are to remain challenged and interested in spiritual things. The final section of this chapter will give you several ideas and teaching methods worth considering.

3. CHURCHIANITY VS. CHRISTIANITY

Have you ever felt like your students' faith is tied more to the activities and ministries of your church than to a growing relationship with Jesus? As I mentioned, young people who have grown up in the church often confuse churchianity (involvement with the institution) with Christianity.

In this instance, a student's "faith" is based solely on the church as a multipurpose community center. Outings, vacations (camps and trips), performing arts (choirs, ensembles, and drama groups), sports, and a host of other involvements become the focal point of Christian participation. At a time when Christian young people should be dealing with their faith in more meaningful ways, some are only concerned with the social club mentality of the church and the Christian life. Christian education specialist Marlene LeFever commented on the change of mentality that *should* occur in Christian teens: "As elementary kids they are members of a club (in speaking of the church). But as teenagers they are no longer interested in club membership—they're interested in club ownership. It's no longer their mother and father's faith. They want their own."[3]

Although this statement is generally true, for some teens the transition from borrowed and reflected faith stages to faith ownership never occurs. They remain stalled in the club mentality where social relationships and church activities take the place of a spiritual relationship and meaningful application of Christianity.

4. OVERALL INFLUENCE OF THE CHURCH

Just as children are influenced by their parents, they are also influenced by their church. Issues such as spiritual disinterest, apathy, and attitudes of rigidity or legalism may have their roots in the church itself. However, while the church may be responsible for fueling some problems, it also promotes a great deal of positive input. Dr. Gene Getz has made this observation of reciprocal relationships within the church in the context of the Sunday School. He said "Sunday School structures usually also affect the overall emphasis of the church. If it's Bible teaching, so goes the

Sunday School. If it's relationships, so goes the Sunday School. The strengths and weaknesses of the Sunday School are the strengths and weaknesses of the church."[4]

Since young people are the products of the Sunday Schools and the Sunday Schools are the products of the churches, then the strengths and weaknesses of the church will usually manifest themselves in the lives of its students. For example, if a particular church stresses Christian service and missions, the youth minister probably will not have much trouble getting her students to support and participate in a local inner-city ministry to the poor.

However, the weaknesses of your particular church can affect your students as well. For example, in a church I served, congregational worship wasn't particularly emphasized. While it seemed everyone enjoyed listening to the choir, when it came to their own worship, people were much less responsive. Weekly, I saw people mouthing the words to hymns without any evidence of celebration, reverence, or meaning.

I come from a background where worship is a real priority. It is therefore my natural inclination to emphasize meaningful worship with my youth groups. In this particular ministry, I provided my teens with what I felt was a quality worship experience complete with a contemporary sound (a worship band), balanced material (fun songs and worshipful praise songs), and appropriate mood and atmosphere.

It was a struggle from the very start. The students had a hard time participating with true feeling and enthusiasm, despite my efforts at encouraging them to do so. They had never entered into meaningful worship or seen it modeled and, as a result, were not accustomed to it. I became frustrated trying to teach those church youth how to worship, and it took me a long time to realize that I was struggling against a weakness in the church itself.

Just as I had to learn in this situation, it is important to acknowledge the particular emphases, strengths, and weaknesses of your church. Knowledge of these areas will help you both to maximize your ministry and minimize your frustration.

CHALLENGES FOR MINISTRY

The following suggestions are meant to stimulate thinking and provide practical tools for dealing with the many issues of the church in relation to church youth. By implementing some of these strategies, you will help your students as they begin to own their faith.

1. PROVIDE OPPORTUNITIES FOR STUDENT INVOLVEMENT

Teens learn an experiential faith when they put the words of their faith into action. Even simple projects like mowing an elderly person's lawn, serving in a soup kitchen, or doing crafts with children at an orphanage can begin to help your students internalize their faith.

Student leadership and peer ministry within your youth group are also great faith builders. Not only do church youth become more interested in the program when they have a part in it, but it stretches their faith as they learn through doing. Because service and student involvement are such an integral part of any successful ministry to church youth, I will address both more fully in the last section of this book.

2. USE CREATIVE TEACHING AND PROGRAMMING

Jim Rayburn, founder of Young Life, once said, "It is a sin to bore kids with the Bible." I don't know about you, but I've sinned more than once in that area by using routine lessons and ill-prepared talks. And believe me, church youth are about the most unsympathetic audience you'll find!

The challenge of teaching these students should only encourage you to work harder to communicate God's Word in more effective and interesting ways. In a recent Search Institute study, Peter Benson surveyed more than 11,000 individuals in 561 randomly selected congregations across the United States. He found that the status quo of Christian education was in real need of reform. Among Benson's top suggestions: Abandon the lecture-only format and train teachers.[5]

These recommendations are nothing new to those of us working with teenagers—but we don't always heed them. It's easier to cut corners in training and fall back on lessons that are more efficient than effective. Implementing more creative teaching methods and training others to do the same is vital if we are to keep kids interested in our programs. Edgar Dale's cone of experiential learning demonstrates the importance of using creativity in teaching the truths of Christ if the message is to be retained.

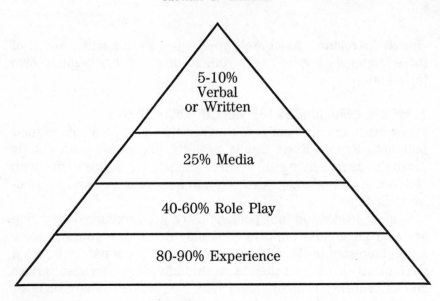

(Percent = Level of Information Retained)

Taken from *The Youth Builder* by Jim Burns, © 1988 by Harvest House
Publishers, Eugene, Oregon 97402. Used by permission.

Traditionally, our teaching methods in Christian education have
been lecture-oriented. Dale suggests that when students are
involved in the learning process, both attention and retention are
increased.[6]

The following alternative teaching methods are designed to involve students in the learning process. Consider how you might
implement one or more of them in your teaching ministry.

- Have students perform a role play of a Bible story or lesson
  subject.
- Use skits or dramatic presentations to complement lessons.
- Give groups of students 15 minutes to come up with a cre-
  ative song, poem, or rap on your lesson theme.
- Have students make a video relating to the teaching topic or
  Bible subject.
- Use case studies and situations that require problem-solving
  to spark discussion.
- Use an interactive (even confrontational) talk show dialogue
  format to promote thinking and discussion.
- Take advantage of small groups to give each student a
  chance to share his or her thoughts, questions, and ideas.

- Let students prepare and make presentations.
- Take creative field trips. For example, visit a mortuary for a discussion on death or go to a mall to talk about materialism.

3. EMPHASIZE THE SPIRITUAL

Remind students that although church attendance and youth group involvement are important, these do not take the place of one's personal relationship with Jesus Christ. When your group meets, don't let your students worship and pray in routine, repetitive fashion. Strive to make the ordinary *extraordinary* by helping them come into contact with God through meaningful prayer, praise, and worship times.

Share answered prayers to alert your students to God's working in their midst. Make worship and singing a priority in your group, rather than a time filler or preliminary exercise. Encourage students to share testimonies to demonstrate to their friends that God is actively working in their lives. Allow students time in small groups to share with one another for accountability, mutual support, and encouragement.

By keeping your focus on the Lord, you'll not only create integrity in your ministry but will continue the process of faith ownership in the lives of your students.

4. DON'T LET YOUR CHURCH'S SITUATION LIMIT YOUR MINISTRY

Although your students will reflect the strengths and weaknesses of your church to a certain extent, you don't necessarily need to be limited by the situation. If your church is strong in the area of Bible teaching, capitalize on that strength by offering chapter-by-chapter studies on a particular book of the Bible. Teach teens to use concordances, Bible dictionaries, and other reference books to increase their knowledge. Don't ignore strengths that are already established in your church. You can capitalize on those strengths to promote Christian growth in the lives of your students.

In terms of your church's weaknesses—whether lack of enthusiasm, lack of evangelistic fervor, or mediocrity in worship—don't despair! God may use your youth group to positively influence the church in an area of needed growth. As history has shown us, if any one group can promote change, it's young people.

THINK ABOUT IT

1. Generally, are you able to recognize the stages of faith development in your young people? For starters, what are some of the basic differences between the faith of junior highers and senior highers? List them below.

Junior Highers	Senior Highers

2. Do you use extrinsic or intrinsic methods, or perhaps a combination, to spiritually motivate your students? When and why do you use each type of motivation?

3. Are church youth ever bored with your youth meetings? Evaluate your teaching style: What percentage is lecture vs. experiential/involvement learning? What can you do to improve the learning process?

4. What aspects of your church's style (practices, emphases, traditions, etc.) affect your youth ministry? What can you do to compensate for these factors and/or use them to the best advantage in your ministry?

NOTES

1. L. Berkhof, *Systematic Theology* (Grand Rapids, Michigan: Wm. B. Eerdmans Publishing Co., 1941), p. 503.
2. Summarized from V. Bailey Gillespie, *The Experience of Faith* (Birmingham, Alabama: Religious Education Press, 1988), pp. 92–155.
3. Marlene LeFever (quote taken from a 1989 *USA Today* article entitled, "Kids Bringing Parents Back to the Faith" by Nanci Hellmich.)
4. Gene Getz, A National Christian Education Study Seminar Report: "The Sunday School Today and Tomorrow" (Wheaton, Illinois: Scripture Press Ministries, 1975), p. 33.
5. Peter Benson, "A Tired Enterprise in Need of Reform," *Youthworker Journal* 6 (Summer 1990): 50.
6. Jim Burns, *The Youth Builder* (Eugene, Oregon: Harvest House Publishers, 1988), pp. 183–184.

STRUGGLES THAT EMERGE

Let's face it—none of us like struggles. Life is so much simpler without them. But they come, don't they? Whether young or old, rich or poor, black or white, they come. Gratefully, as Christians we at least have an idea of why we face struggles and trials in our lives. Remember James 1:2-4? "Consider it all joy, my brethren, when you encounter various trials, knowing that the testing of your faith produces endurance. And let endurance have its perfect result, that you may be perfect and complete, lacking in nothing."

Struggles, or trials, are part of God's training program to produce faith and spiritual endurance in the lives of His children. Now, take that truth and apply it to the students in your group who have grown up in the church. As we have seen, because of their backgrounds, they face very specific challenges that are common to many of them. For example, unlike their counterparts from non-Christian homes, they struggle as much with what they *haven't* done wrong or right as with what they *have*. By understanding the challenges they face, you can better help your students work through these struggles and achieve spiritual victory rather than defeat.

CHAPTER FOUR

MEASURING UP TO CHRISTIAN STANDARDS

The young man who sat in my office one afternoon in February was searching for a shoulder to cry on. I considered Kevin to be one of the strongest spiritual leaders in my youth group; but as we talked, I realized he was feeling weak and spiritually defeated. With tears in his eyes, Kevin told me the Christian life was just too tough to pull off.

"All my life I've been taught what's right and wrong. I know from God's Word what He expects of me, but I just can't seem to live up to His standards." Kevin went on to lament, "When my non-Christian friends 'make it' with a girl, they broadcast it throughout the entire guys' locker room. When I go so far as to touch a girl the wrong way, my conscience won't let up. The guilt gets so heavy sometimes I feel it's going to crush me. If being a Christian is supposed to be joyful, why am I so miserable?"

For most teens, it's difficult enough to have to meet the standards and expectations of everyday adolescent life. But church youth also face the daily challenge of spiritual demands. In general, young people are bombarded with ideals from the media that stress slim bodies, perfect tans, straight teeth, clear complexions, and designer clothing. Add to that the expectations of most parents which usually include good grades, good friends, and good behavior. Good grief! That list by itself frustrates the majority of adolescents. But add to that the responsibility of adhering to the spiritual, moral, and ethical teachings of Scripture (administered by parents and Sunday School teachers alike), and you've got quite a tall order to fill.

Jim Long, senior editor of *Campus Life* magazine, captured the struggle that many church youth encounter in his poem "Moral Marksman."

> Targets are fun things.
> Round
> with circles
> inside circles
> and a dot in the middle.
>
> I'd like to think
> I could bend the bow,
> let an arrow fly
> and pierce the dot
> dead center,
> the arrow vibrating
> with a nice
> solid
> twang.
>
> So
> what are these arrows doing
> stuck and standing
> pin-cushion like
> in the ground,
> on trees,
> everywhere
> but where I aim them?

What is this
unseen force field,
surrounding these concentric circles,
keeping the target
free from puncture?

Targets are fun things.
Missing them is a drag.[1]

MISSING THE MARK

The Greek word for sin (*hamartia*) literally means to "miss the mark" and was a phrase used to describe an archer missing the bull's-eye of his target. When a miss occurred, the archer was said to have committed a sin. The New Testament writers borrowed this concept to illustrate how God's children often fall short of their Heavenly Father's bull's-eye for Christian faith and practice.

God's standards for spiritual, moral, and ethical behavior are set in Scripture, giving us a definite target at which to aim. Unfortunately, Christian marksmanship is a difficult feat to master. For many nonchurched Christian kids, the problem is more often getting them to recognize the standards and establish Christian lifestyles. However, church youth know where the target stands. Its position is etched firmly in their sights. But not only can missing it be a drag, it can get downright discouraging!

Put yourself in a Christian teenager's shoes for a minute. Feel familiar? Gym socks rolled down to the ankles in well-worn high tops with the laces undone. You're 16 years old and from an average Christian family. You're on the basketball team, active in the youth group, like to date, and have a part-time job. You're one busy guy. But hey, who isn't? You do your best to please God and your family, but it's usually an uphill battle. There's so much pressure to conform at school. But you know what's right. It's been told to you at least a thousand times:

- Christians are honest; they don't cheat at school or lie to their parents.
- Christians forgive; they don't hold grudges, get even, or turn bitter.
- Christians are morally upright; they treat the opposite sex with respect and don't get too involved physically. They stay away from movies with sex, bad language, and violence. They

are very selective with the music they listen to; most of it is lyrically appropriate.

- Christians obey their parents and attempt to get along with their brothers and sisters.
- Christians witness to their unsaved friends.
- Christians desire to serve God and other people, especially those less fortunate.
- Christians have a daily time alone with God that might include prayer or Bible study.
- Christians are active in church programs and corporate worship.
- Christians obey their authority figures, including parents, teachers, coaches, ministers, and police.
- Christians cultivate a growing faith and trust in God.
- Christians don't swear, gossip, or cause strife.
- Christians are humble, not selfish and prideful.

And the list goes on . . .

Now my intention is not to reduce the teachings and admonitions of Scripture to a list of do's and don'ts but to point out the way many church youth view the expectations of their faith. Being a Christian teenager is a tough job. Even with the help of the Holy Spirit, it takes a lot of effort, sweat, and tears to live the sanctified life. And unfortunately, the target can't be hit all the time. When arrows miss the mark, some try harder. Others get frustrated, worried, and depressed, wondering to themselves, *Shouldn't I be getting better after all this time?*

Like the Workaholic Worrywart described in chapter 1, the sincere Christian young person can easily become confused and dejected trying to live a faith that, to them, seems next to impossible. As in John Bunyan's *Pilgrim's Progress*, the "Slough of Despond" will always be waiting to slow a Christian's pace. There will always be characters such as Mr. Worldly Wiseman, attempting to distract and alter a Christian's course, while foes such as Legality, Ignorance, and Hypocrisy work to confuse the Christian.

Bunyan's classic similitude of the Christian pilgrimage from birth to glory depicts the triumphs and tragedies encountered along the way toward Christian maturity. As Bunyan's story so aptly illustrates, targets will be missed along the way and falls will occur, but the end of the journey is well worth it.

TAKING THE FALL

Church youth struggle to live the Christian life in a variety of ways. And like all of us, they fail from time to time. I've heard many young people tell me how sinful and frustrated they've felt after seeing a movie they *knew* they shouldn't have seen or bought an album that no Christian should have any business listening to. Some cheat at school while others lie to their parents. There are also those who fall to the temptation of drugs and alcohol, later regretting their actions in light of their Christian faith.

SEXUAL SINS

Perhaps one of the most difficult areas for these teens to maintain is their sexual standards. Each year they hear sex and dating talks from youth workers, correctly urging them to abstain from sexual immorality (1 Thessalonians 4:3). Preachers and parents communicate the same message too. Yet try as they may to avoid sexual involvement and listen to the advice of their counselors, there are other voices convincing them to indulge. And they often do.

For example, a recent study indicated that "media (TV, radio, movies) ranks third, behind peers and parents, in influencing the values and behavior of teens—Christian or otherwise. This represents a dramatic shift since 1960 when media ranked eighth behind such factors as teachers, relatives and religious leaders."[2] In terms of sexual conduct, the media is filling our students' minds with nothing but lies.

Josh McDowell and Dick Day, in their excellent book on teen sexuality, *Why Wait?* reported a study that estimated that the average person views over 9,230 sex acts per year on television. Of those sexual acts, 81 per cent are depicted outside of marriage. After 10 years of average television viewing, a young person between the ages of 8 and 18 will see 72,900 scenes of premarital sex or extramarital affairs.[3]

The popular opinion of many youth workers today is that Satan uses the media as his most effective tool for destroying the lives of Christian young people in the area of sexuality. In a survey of 1,400 conservative Christian teenagers, 43 per cent of 18-year-olds admitted to having premarital sexual intercourse.[4] That figure is not far from the national average for youth in general.

This battle is exemplified by a letter I received from a former student:

> Jennifer and I blew it again on our last date—we even prayed for [physical] control before we went out, but it didn't work. We fell to the same old desires and temptations we always do and we both feel terrible after we've gone too far. You know we love the Lord and wish to serve Him, but you also know how much we care for one another. Sometimes we feel like giving up on God, since we can't please Him anyway. But we really don't want to do that. What can we do?

There are, of course, many words of advice a youth worker might offer in counseling these young people. Oftentimes a tough approach is called for. I would likely counsel this couple to break up. However, remember that understanding, patience, and encouragement are also needed to communicate your support and love.

Michel Quoist has captured the struggle many face in this prayer:

I have fallen, Lord,
Once more.
I can't go on, I'll never succeed.
I am ashamed, I don't dare look at you.

. . . .

But temptation blew like a hurricane,
And instead of looking at you I turned my head away
I stepped aside
While you stood, silent and sorrowful.

. . . .

This sin that I have wanted but want no more,
that I have imagined,
      sought,
      played with,
      fondled
   for a long time;
That I have finally embraced while turning coldly away from you.

. . . .

And the Lord will answer:

> Come, son, look up.
> Isn't it mainly your vanity that is wounded?
> If you loved me, you would grieve, but you would trust.
>
> . . . .
>
> Ask my pardon
> And get up quickly.
> You see, it's not falling that is the worst,
> But staying on the ground![5]

SINS OF OMISSION

Another major domain in which church youth struggle to maintain Christian standards is in the area of sins of omission. James 4:17 describes it plainly: "To one who knows the right thing to do, and does not do it, to him it is sin."

Although in context James admonished Christians against worldliness and arrogance, the concept might readily apply to other scriptural expectations as well. On the one hand, adolescents are sensitized to sins of commission—tangible displays of disobedience, such as lying, stealing, and acts of immorality. On the other hand, church youth are also aware of the responsibilities given in Scripture that they have not even attempted to carry out—sins of omission. Biblical standards, such as Christian service, personal prayer, Bible reading, evangelism, and social action can be included in this category.

Time and again I've had conversations with teens who sincerely struggle in this area. Eric, a senior in high school, exclaimed, "My friends are all going to hell, and I'm not doing a thing about it. I know I'm called to be a witness, but I don't. What must God think of me?"

Julie, a junior higher, once said to me in response to going on a service trip to Mexico, "I've already made plans to go to the mall on Saturday. Besides, who wants to get all dirty and smelly in Mexico? Do you think God will be mad at me?"

Duane was a sophomore who struggled with having a consistent time alone with God. He said, "I just can't seem to take time to read my Bible and pray on my own. I have no motivation or desire, even though I know God wants me to."

The pressures to obey *all* of God's revelation in His Word can be psychologically, emotionally, and spiritually overwhelming at times for Christian youth. As students grow in their relationships with Christ, the Holy Spirit will motivate them more and more to make these activities part of their lives. But as they grow, they need constant encouragement, admonition, and support—as well as a little grace now and then.

BIBLICAL EXAMPLES

Church youth need to know that they're not the only ones who struggle spiritually. In fact, an overview of the Bible from cover to cover reveals that many faltered along the way in meeting God's expectations. You only have to turn a page or two in Genesis to find the account of Adam and Eve's fall from grace as they disobeyed God in the Garden (Genesis 3:1-24).

While God was giving Moses the Law, it was none other than God's chosen priest and Moses' brother, Aaron, who led the people in their idolatrous worship of the golden calf (Exodus 32:15-35). Moving through biblical history, we encounter Israel's first king, Saul, who impatiently delivered the burnt offering to unite his people and prepare for war with the Philistines while he should have waited for God's anointed prophet, Samuel (1 Samuel 13:8-14).

And don't forget David, the man after God's own heart, who gave in to the temptation of lust when he involved himself with Bathsheba (2 Samuel 11). His son and successor, Solomon, stumbled too. In the beginning, his reign was characterized by wisdom but ended with foolishness and defiance in God's sight (1 Kings 11:1-11).

The New Testament offers us several examples too. Although Peter led the disciples in establishing the church (Acts 2), remember it was also this same individual who boldly declared to Jesus that he would never abandon or forsake Him. Yet Peter denied his Savior just as predicted (Luke 22:31-34, 54-62). Paul, the great missionary of the church, admitted to struggling with missing the mark: "For that which I am doing, I do not understand; for I am not practicing what I would like to do, but I am doing the very thing I hate" (Romans 7:15).

Then there were the Corinthians—an entire congregation who failed to live up to the Christian standards taught them. Finally, remember the situation of the church in Laodicea, a group of lukewarm Christians in whom God was obviously disappointed (Revelation 3:14-22).

My point is not to condone such acts. Rather, I want to point out that throughout biblical history, God's followers have known His will and standards and yet many have struggled with them. Church youth need to know that they are not alone in their quests for spiritual progress.

CONSEQUENCES

For every action there is some type of reaction. A pitcher throws the ball (action) and the batter attempts to hit it (reaction). And it follows that with every reaction, there will be some type of consequence or result. If the batter swings and misses the ball, it will be a strike against him. However, if he makes contact, he may get a base hit.

Similarly, God has acted by revealing His divine will to us in Scripture. People will react to God in one way or another, although His standards are the same for everyone. For church youth, reacting to God's revelation (His Word) in obedience and faith usually results in a growing relationship with the Lord. However, when they fall, the consequences can be painful and sometimes spiritually damaging. How teens respond to their spiritual falls can make the difference between growth or disillusionment.

GUILT

Guilt is a feeling God never intended humankind to experience. Yet man fell in the Garden and the "fruits" of sin became manifest to all succeeding generations (Romans 5:12). Guilt is a result of sin. When Adam and Eve disobeyed God, ate of the fruit, and received the knowledge of good and evil, they immediately experienced the consequences of shame and guilt. As a result, the two covered their nakedness and hid themselves from God (Genesis 3:6-8). Sadly, the human race has been repeating the process ever since.

Christian teens are not immune from feelings of guilt. S. Rickly Christian noted in one of his popular teen devotionals, "Because we're imperfect human beings, we'll never be free from the weight of guilt. It's there to remind us when we fall short of God's standards. Yet God is not some cosmic madman who delights in watching us squirm."[6]

However, squirm they do. And usually much more than their non-Christian friends because their standards are higher—and they *know* it! The tender conscience of a Christian teen is a vulnerable thing indeed. Feelings of guilt can either convict or condemn. In the positive sense, the Holy Spirit uses conviction to motivate young people to repentance and positive action.

When guilt is followed by confession and repentance, joy and fellowship are restored with God through forgiveness. But guilt can work in a negative way too. The conscience is not an infallible mechanism and can often become unreliable; self-condemnation can be the result. As Dr. James Dobson commented, "By setting an ethical standard which is impossible to maintain, Satan can generate severe feelings of condemnation and spiritual discouragement. . . . Some feelings of guilt are obviously inspired by the devil and have nothing to do with the commandments, values or judgments of our Creator."[7]

Satan's condemnation can lead church youth to confusion, frustration, despair, and feelings of hopelessness, pushing them further and further away from their Heavenly Father who loves them. When young people who have known of God's love all their lives blow it, Satan often will produce feelings of accusatory false guilt that go far beyond biblical conviction. Such statements as the following are not from God: "You're worthless. You're a failure. I told you so. How can you call yourself a Christian? Nobody loves you. You're a loser. Give up!" Therefore, it is crucial that youth workers assist church youth in discerning the voices of their consciences and whether they are working for or against them.

RESENTMENT

When I think of how some Christians end up resenting God, I am always drawn to the story of Cain. His is an unfortunate example of a man who allowed the seeds of discouragement to fester and grow into the roots of resentment. And those roots grew to a point where his relationship with God was ruined.

Genesis 4:1-4 tells us that Eve gave birth to two sons, Cain and Abel. Cain was a farmer and his younger brother Abel, a keeper of flocks. Both desired to please God and find favor in His sight; however, the Lord regarded only Abel's offering as acceptable. Verse 5 says that Cain's offering was rejected by God for some reason and, as a result, Cain became very angry and discouraged.

God's response to Cain was, "Why are you angry? And why has your countenance fallen? If you do well, will not your countenance be lifted up? And if you do not do well, sin is crouching at the door; and its desire is for you, but you must master it" (v. 6).

Cain wasn't excited about God's counsel. In fact, he resented God because he felt he couldn't meet His standards and expectations. Instead of learning from his mistakes, Cain allowed his discouragement to breed resentment and contempt for God. And, as you know, he took it out on his brother Abel!

Although the situations are different, Christian youth often struggle with the same kind of resentment that plagued Cain. Whether the pressures come from church, family, teachers, or within themselves, these students perceive that they can never measure up to the standards God has for them. After repeated failure, I've known students to literally want to give up and simply stop trying.

Lisa was a high schooler who grew up in a Christian home and was active in our youth group. But deep down, Lisa had bitter feelings toward God. She had witnessed her grandfather struggle in the ministry and almost lose his faith while having to live with her Christian parents whose marriage was on the rocks. Lisa herself had gotten involved in the party scene and was struggling spiritually. She concluded that since her own family couldn't live a genuine faith, then neither could she. God was more of a home wrecker than a caring and compassionate Father, and Lisa blamed Him for her family's unhappiness. Her resentment led to actions of open rebellion against God as she willingly hid her pain in drugs and alcohol. Like Cain, she felt she could never live up to God's expectations for her. Instead of learning from her mistakes and the struggles of her family, she allowed herself to turn bitter.

DEPRESSION AND DISCOURAGEMENT

When guilt feelings are not properly addressed, depression can result. Just as an adult can get depressed and discouraged over a failed business venture or a troubled marriage, so too can a Christian adolescent experience depression and spiritual discouragement over what he or she might consider to be a failed relationship with God.

For example, the following is the account of a former youth pastor who struggled in this same area:

There was a time in my life when I fell away from the Lord badly, shamefully. And I felt God would never be able to use [me] again in any small way. I didn't know how to handle my failure. I didn't know how to get close to God.

Even after I read the Bible to see what God had to say about my dilemma, I still felt I had to crucify myself. Somehow I had to prove my sorrow by knocking my head against a wall and saying, "I'm sorry! I'm sorry! See how sorry I am, Lord? I'll crucify myself! See?"

During this period a friend came to me and said, "We need somebody to lead a little Bible study with a few kids in the community. Would you consider . . ."

"Oh no," I said. "Not me. You know about me. You know how I fell away from the Lord. I couldn't."[8]

The young man's friend went on to explain to him that Christ had already been crucified on the cross so that he wouldn't have to. He encouraged him to give his depression and discouragement to God so that he could continue to grow in his walk and be used again by God. Those words of timely counsel made a powerful impact on that young man. He went on to grow that little Bible study into a successful youth program of hundreds. He eventually began Willow Creek Community Church in a northwest suburb of Chicago, which is now one of the largest congregations in the country. That former youth worker is Bill Hybels.

APATHY

Finally, some church youth simply get tired of trying to live as God intended and become apathetic or complacent with their faith. Others I've encountered respond in quite the opposite way, living in fear rather than faith. A junior in high school once told me that she was scared of losing her salvation with every sin she committed or every command she did not obey.

Overall, students need to realize, accept, and understand that falls *will* occur in the Christian life *all the time*. But like a determined boxer who refuses to stay down, they must continue to get up!

WAYS TO MEASURE UP

Here are several ways to encourage your students to grow in their relationships with the Lord, despite standards and setbacks.

MANAGING TIP #1—
GOD'S ACCEPTANCE IS BASED ON LOVE, NOT PERFORMANCE

The problem we have addressed in this chapter actually deals with a false assumption many church youth have come to believe: God accepts us more or less depending on whether or not we perform to His standards. It is true that in a very practical sense we are "created in Christ Jesus for good works, which God prepared beforehand, that we should walk in them" (Ephesians 2:10). Good works, or doing all that is commanded in Scripture, does not determine our approval rating before God. In fact, Paul makes this perfectly clear in the verses preceding the one just quoted: "For by grace you have been saved through faith; and that not of yourselves, it is the gift of God; not as a result of works, that no one should boast" (Ephesians 2:8-9).

Then how are sincere Christian young people who disappoint God and sin daily to be assured that God still loves them? Answer: God's love is unconditional—no strings attached! First John 4:10 tells us, "In this is love, not that we loved God, but that He loved us and sent His Son to be the propitiation for our sins."

God's great and boundless love for us sent His only Son to the cross. There is nothing you or I could have ever done to merit this act. Why then should an *act* we do or don't do merit any more or less of His acceptance? Struggling Christian youth need the assurance that truly nothing can "separate us from the love of God, which is in Christ Jesus" (Romans 8:39).

MANAGING TIP #2—THE STANDARD IS PROGRESS, NOT PERFECTION

In 1980, George Brett attempted to become the first baseball player since Ted Williams to bat .400 for a season. That year, Brett captivated the interest of many Americans—serious fan and casual observer alike—as he pursued his quest for Williams' mark. After all, this challenge is quite a feat. To hit .400, or in other words to hit safely 40 percent of the time, is considered phenomenal. Think about it: As an extremely gifted and talented batter, you are allowed to fail 6 out of 10 times.[9] I call that accentuating the positive!

Lesson to be learned: Help your students focus on the positive ways they're growing in their faith, not the negative. The Christian life is filled with peaks and valleys. There will be spiritual highs and lows as young Christians grow in sanctification. Encourage them as they mature in the Lord by allowing for failure now and then. Model the Apostle Paul's attitude:

> Not that I have already obtained *it,* or have already become perfect, but I press on in order that I may lay hold of that for which also I was laid hold of by Christ Jesus. Brethren, I do not regard myself as having laid hold of it yet; but one thing *I do:* forgetting what *lies* behind and reaching forward to what *lies* ahead, I press on toward the goal for the prize of the upward call of God in Christ Jesus.
>
> (Philippians 3:12-14)

Secondly, reassure them that even when they fail, God is still at work in their lives to bring about His will for them (Philippians 2:13). When they feel like giving up, encourage them to "press on toward the goal to win the prize for which God has called me heavenward in Christ Jesus" (Philippians 3:14, NIV).

Finally, remind students that only Jesus was able to measure up to His Heavenly Father's standards and expectations perfectly and without sin (Hebrews 4:15). He also knows what they're going through because He's been there.

By the way . . . George Brett never made it to .400.

MANAGING TIP #3—FOULED UP, BUT FORGIVEN

Sometime during World War II, a frustrated sailor signaled to his superior officer a response which many of us can relate to: "Situation Normal: All Fouled Up." Before too long, the word *snafu* entered the American vocabulary.[10] It works OK in a Christian vocabulary too!

Growing up as a Christian teenager I had a lot of those spiritual snafu-type days. No matter how hard I tried to do right, in the end I managed to foul things up pretty well. But that's why Jesus came in the first place. Whether "born believers" or not, we still have sin natures that tend to foul us up spiritually—situation normal. That description might be how some of your students feel; but emphasize that through confession and repentance, sin is forgiven by God. Here are several Scriptures that include God's promise of forgiveness:

> If we confess our sins, He is faithful and righteous to forgive us our sins and to cleanse us from all unrighteousness.
>
> (1 John 1:9)

As far as the east is from the west, so far has He removed our transgressions from us.

(Psalm 103:12)

Though your sins are as scarlet, they will be as white as snow; though they are red like crimson, they will be like wool.

(Isaiah 1:18)

I like the old bumper sticker that reads, "Christians aren't perfect . . . just forgiven." That simple truth sums up in one sentence what church youth need to hear most when their spiritual situations are all fouled up. God's incomparable gift of forgiveness is waiting to be taken; encourage your students to receive it.

Finally, in all this talk of grace and forgiveness, we cannot forget that Christian young people *are* to strive for obedience and Christian maturity, even if that quest is difficult. God has given us a standard of holiness, and it's a standard we should strive for, not out of fear or a desire to please parents or church leaders but out of love and gratitude to God. "What shall we say then? Are we to continue in sin that grace might increase? May it never be! How shall we who died to sin still live in it?" (Romans 6:1-2).

THINK ABOUT IT

1. How do you rate in communicating your own spiritual struggles and failures to your students? Check the most appropriate response.
   (a) I'm honest and transparent with them.
   (b) I try not to mention my faults.
   (c) I'm usually guarded but open up occasionally.

2. Does your teaching style tend to be more forgiving or judgmental? Do you motivate students with encouragement or fear? Why?

3. Think of a particular student in your group who is struggling with a performance mind-set in terms of living the Christian life. What can you say this week to encourage him or her?

4. How well do you measure up to Christian standards in your own life?

5. Pray that your students will grow in their relationships with the Lord, living in faith rather than fear.

NOTES

1. Jim Long, *LifeQuest* (Wheaton, Illinois: Tyndale House Publishers, 1988), pp. 57–58.
2. The Robert Johnston Company, Inc., "The Teen Environment," in *Why Wait?* Josh McDowell and Dick Day (San Bernardino, California: Here's Life Publishers, 1957) p. 40.
3. Josh McDowell and Dick Day, *Why Wait?* (San Bernardino, California: Here's Life Publishers, 1987), p. 40.
4. Josh McDowell Ministry, *Teen Sex Survey in the Evangelical Church: Executive Summary Report* in *The Youth Ministry Resource Book*, ed. Eugene C. Roehlkepartain, (Loveland, Colorado: Group Books, 1988), p. 51.
5. Michel Quoist, *Prayers* (New York: Sheed and Ward, Inc., 1963), pp. 135–137.
6. S. Rickly Christian, *Alive* (Grand Rapids, Michigan: Zondervan Publishing House, 1990), p. 243.
7. Dr. James Dobson, *Emotions: Can You Trust Them?* (Ventura, California: Regal Books, 1980), pp. 20–21.
8. Bill Hybels, *Caution: Christians Under Construction* (Wheaton, Illinois: Victor Books, 1978), pp. 66–67.
9. Earl D. Wilson, *Try Being a Teenager* (Portland, Oregon: Multnomah Press, 1982), p. 123.
10. Harold Myra, *The New You* (Wheaton, Illinois: Victor Books, 1980), p. 87.

CHAPTER FIVE

CONVERSION AND CONVERTING

I'll never forget the time in high school when I heard the testimony of Darrell Mansfield. The long-haired musician came to do a concert for our youth group at our midweek Bible study. The man who stood before us that night had come to the Lord in a most dramatic way. But I think it was Darrell's genuine love for his Savior that impacted me most that night.

We all sat silently as he told his story, hanging onto his every word. Darrell had grown up in the '60s amidst the Vietnam War and the drug culture. He grew increasingly unhappy with life, and several tragic events occurred that drove him to desperation in his search for real peace and love. One of his best friends died of a heroin overdose. Another was killed in the Vietnam War. Both of Darrell's parents were alcoholics, and they divorced while Darrell was still in high school. Finally his grandfather, whom he loved very much and looked to for love and support, died suddenly.

In a last desperate attempt to give his life meaning and purpose, Mansfield chose to give himself totally to God in the only way he knew how. One lonely night, he went to the church building he had grown up in. Helplessly he said, "Here I am, Lord, take me." Laying at the altar, he slit both his wrists with a butcher knife. He was 21 years old.

By God's grace, a clergyman happened into the building and summoned the police and an ambulance. Darrell was rushed to the hospital, and his life was spared. Through the testimony of a friend's family, Darrell came to understand how to really give his life to God; and he entered into a relationship with Jesus Christ.

We sat in stunned amazement at hearing the rocker's dynamic testimony. This was a totally radical, "No way!" experience to us sheltered church kids. We were hardly willing to sacrifice a Saturday to visit the elderly, let alone sacrifice our lives for God. Although Mansfield's experience with radical salvation was truly inspiring, in all reality it was difficult for many of us to relate to. It even caused some of us to take a dim view of our own uneventful conversions.

STRUGGLES CHURCH YOUTH FACE

Church youth face several struggles when dealing with the subjects of conversion and evangelism.

1. GRAY TESTIMONIES

Darrell's conversion experience might easily be described as a black-and-white scenario. Darrell experienced definite changes in mind-set, attitude, and behavior after his conversion. However, this is not the common experience of most youth who have grown up in the church. Being raised in an ever-present environment of Christianity, most have simply "oozed" into a relationship with the Lord that was neither dramatic nor all that life changing. Not black, nor white, but shades of gray.

Webster defines gray as "intermediate in position, condition, or character"; in other words, vague. I have found this definition helpful in understanding how many church youth feel about their testimonies. At Christian concerts, camps, and rallies, teens hear radical, black-and-white models of Christian testimonies. However, when I asked a group of church youth the question, "How was your life different before and after you became a Christian?" their responses were very different.

- "I became a Christian when I was in grade school. I guess there was never a real big change." *Brian, age 17*
- "I've known the Lord all my life. I've never really been bad, but never really 'on fire' either." *Denise, age 16*
- "I think I was always just expected to accept Christianity. There was no 'before' and 'after.' " *John, age 16*
- "Before I made a personal decision for Christ, I was pretty disrespectful to my parents. After I became a Christian, I tried to do better, but still blew it a lot." *Jill, age 15*

As a high school student, I remember a camp speaker saying to us, "Young people, if you can't recount the exact experience of your conversion from darkness into light—the date, time, and place—then you've probably never been saved." That kind of pressure is a heavy load to place on an adolescent who grew up in the church and spent his whole life in Sunday School. Too often, however, young people are overexposed to this kind of challenge.

Veteran youth worker and author Denny Rydberg has the kind of testimony youth need to hear now and then for the sake of balance and reality.

I grew up in a home where Christ was honored and where the Bible was held in highest esteem.

When I was little, we had family devotions (Mom, Dad, and my two brothers). Mom would play the piano and lead singing, Dad would read a Bible story, and we would all pray. Sometimes we liked family devotions; sometimes we didn't. But that didn't matter. Attendance was mandatory.

We attended a Baptist church. . . . The Sunday school teachers were sincere but generally the youth program wasn't anything to write home about. . . .

When I was eight years old, I marched down the aisle on the night of the daily vacation Bible school program and gave my life to Christ. I was sincere but as I grew older, my faith grew colder. Once in a while, it would become exciting for me, but most of the time—

in junior high and high school—I went through the motions because they were expected of me. . . .

In my senior year in high school, I encountered Jesus Christ in a fresh way and realized that if I was going to live the Christian life, I couldn't do it on my own. I needed to rely on the power of Christ—the Holy Spirit—to succeed. And I began to trust God more for His daily direction and power in my life.[1]

2. COMPARISON

Comparison is perhaps one of the devil's most potent poisons—even when taken in small doses. Comparison is an enemy we all struggle with, a temptation that can either fill us with pride or break us through discouragement. However, when it comes to testimonies, we all need to take a realistic look at the content before we overglorify the speaker or hold him up for comparison. We've all heard testimonies that seem to stray from the grace of God to the boastings of men. A former pastor of mine, Chuck Swindoll, likes to refer to them as "braggamonies."

On the other hand, I've encountered many church youth discouraged by their bland and ordinary conversion experiences when compared to others. Christian celebrities, dynamic circuit speakers, and contemporary Christian rock stars who have extraordinary testimonies can be very successful in converting, challenging, and encouraging young people to take God more seriously.

However, some church youth may get discouraged and confused as they grapple with their own average Christian experiences. Statements such as, "I wish I had an awesome testimony like that" or "How come my conversion was so boring?" commonly emerge from these comparisons.

Solutions are not easily found. Popular Christian films and books commonly portray the more exciting conversion stories of ex-drug addicts, gang members, convicts, and satanists. While they are inspiring, they also provide church youth opportunities for undue comparison and self-doubt.

Even the Bible offers a dramatic and unbelievable testimony that might have been cause for a few unhealthy comparisons. Allow me to take you back to the first century A.D. as the Apostle Paul shared his remarkable testimony before a hostile crowd in Jerusalem.

I am a Jew, born in Tarsus of Cilicia, but brought up in this city, educated under Gamaliel, strictly according to the law of our fathers, being zealous for God, just as you all are today. And I persecuted this Way to the death, binding and putting both men and women into prisons, as also the high priest and all the Council of the elders can testify. From them I also received letters to the brethren, and started off for Damascus in order to bring even those who were there to Jerusalem as prisoners to be punished.

And it came about that as I was on my way, approaching Damascus about noontime, a very bright light suddenly flashed from heaven all around me, and I fell to the ground and heard a voice saying to me, "Saul, Saul, why are you persecuting Me?" And I answered, "Who art Thou, Lord?" And He said to me, "I am Jesus the Nazarene, whom you are persecuting." And those who were with me beheld the light, to be sure, but did not understand the voice of the One who was speaking to me. And I said, "What shall I do, Lord?" And the Lord said to me, "Arise and go into Damascus; and there you will be told of all that has been appointed for you to do." But since I could not see because of the brightness of that light, I was led by the hand by those who were with me, and came into Damascus.

And a certain Ananias, a man who was devout by the standard of the Law, and well spoken of by all the Jews who lived there, came to me, and standing near said to me, "Brother Saul, receive your sight!" And at that very time I looked up at him. And he said, "The God of our fathers has appointed you to know His will, and to see the Righteous One, and to hear an utterance from His mouth. For you will be a witness for Him to all men of what you have seen and heard. And now why do you delay? Arise, and be baptized, and wash away your sins, calling on His name."

(Acts 22:3-16)

Now there's a radical conversion! But as we will see, even the most ordinary student has an exciting and valid story when it's *God* at work in his or her life. However, before we go on to that, let's take a look at another common conflict facing church youth.

3. AVERSION TO CONVERSION
Related to the testimony, another struggle many church youth seem to experience is difficulty in sharing their faith. However, this shouldn't come as a surprise since most of their parents struggle too. Author and evangelist Joseph Aldrich has found that

"only about 10 percent of believers are gifted to share Christ using the methods presented in almost 100 percent of the classes on personal evangelism."[2] Aldrich's goal is to motivate and unleash the other 90 percent to begin the process of effective evangelism. I'm sure most of us working with youth share his desire.

Still, it is beneficial to consider the various stumbling blocks young people face when witnessing to their unsaved friends. First, although Scripture directs all Christians to be involved in the work of evangelism (Matthew 28:18-20), Christians who have grown up in the faith (second, third, etc. generation Christians) tend to lack the evangelistic zeal and fervor of first generation converts. Not only has this problem been recognized by church growth experts and others, but it is a familiar pattern in biblical history as well.

For example, consider the case of Joshua's generation in Old Testament times. They witnessed firsthand God's mighty deeds and power as the Children of Israel conquered and occupied the Promised Land. This first generation, so to speak, received God's promise of the land and committed themselves to serve only Him, rather than the idol gods of the new land (Joshua 24:1-28). Their faith, zeal, and dedication to God were based on personal experience with radical change and manifest power.

However, the spiritual strength and vitality which characterized Joshua's generation did not automatically pass to succeeding generations. Their experiences with the faith were second hand and, although equally significant, lacking in conviction and zeal. In fact, many abandoned their parents' God altogether (Judges 2:6-13). Therefore, it is imperative that youth workers challenge students to have firsthand experiences with God that are both exciting and stimulating. (We'll examine specifics in later chapters.) Only then will a personalized faith be transformed into a faith-sharing lifestyle. As one youth evangelist put it, "Evangelism springs from the vitality of our relationship with God."[3]

A second reason church youth exhibit an aversion to conversion is fear. There are many fears that a would-be teen evangelist faces, such as

- lack of ability
- lack of opportunity
- fear of offending
- lack of desire/motivation
- fear of failure.

All of these are valid concerns that many adults experience too. The Apostle Paul, great evangelist that he was, even admitted to being afraid as he initially shared the Gospel with the Corinthians (1 Corinthians 2:1-5). But Paul was able to overcome his fears with a steadfast faith and trust in the power of God. And this can be true for your students as well!

STRATEGIES TO ENCOURAGE AND ENERGIZE

Each student has the capacity to share his or her own faith with confidence and security when encouraged, taught, and properly motivated. The following strategies are designed to provide students with security in their own personal testimonies in order that they may gain the confidence to share with others.

1. REASSURE THAT A CHRISTIAN HOME IS A PRIVILEGE
As mentioned in earlier chapters, it's important that church youth realize the privilege they have in being raised Christian. Let them know they're in good company too. Timothy was a third generation Christian whose faith and commitment to Christ and His church was admired by none less than the "radical" Apostle Paul (2 Timothy 1:5). Although Timothy's specific testimony is never described in Scripture, it is pretty clear that his conversion experience was nurtured in the home—and that's a far cry from Paul's Damascus road.

While a Sunday School conversion at a young age may not be the most dramatic experience, it is a significant privilege nonetheless. The security, knowledge, confidence, and hope the young believer has is a valued treasure many "late bloomers" of the faith may envy. Many would gladly forfeit the scars, struggles, mistakes, and pains of years apart from God in exchange for having known Jesus Christ in earlier years. Such was the case of one of baseball's all-time greats.

He "played 3,033 games and for 12 years led the American League in batting average. For four years, he batted over .400. On his deathbed, July 17, 1961 [after a lifetime of being a notorious troublemaker], he accepted Jesus Christ as his Saviour. He said, 'You tell the boys I'm sorry it was the last part of the ninth that I came to know Christ. I wish it had taken place in the first half of the first.' " His name was Ty Cobb.[4]

75

2. PROMOTE THE IMPORTANCE OF THEIR TESTIMONIES

Church youth need to understand and believe that their personal testimony is valid and vitally important. First, help them realize that God comes to people in different ways. To be sure, they will encounter those who used to be high on drugs who are now "high" on the Lord or those who overcame tremendous odds and circumstances in their quests for eternal life. However, they must learn to accept and cherish the validity of their own salvation experiences—no matter how average they may feel. After all, no encounter with the divine, Almighty God could be, by any standard, considered average.

Psalm 139:13-16 tells us that God skillfully created each of us in an individual manner and that our Heavenly Father has ordained all the days of our lives. Surely the uniqueness of our physical births enlightens us to the significance of our own unique and genuine spiritual births as well.

From this understanding, then, comparisons are completely unnecessary, even harmful. So help students realize that God is proud of their lifelong commitment to Him and that it is Satan who would cause them to doubt, question, and devalue their conversion experience. Remind them that it is actually the church youth, not the radical converts, who have faced the tougher challenges. While many of their counterparts have come to Christ after years of sinful living, they have had to withstand the temptations of their teen years.

Encourage your students to take confidence in the testimonies of how God made a difference in *their* lives, rather than comparing what God did for someone else. Not only will their self-esteem and security be enhanced, but you will also motivate them to share their testimonies.

This motivation leads to a final point: God has given each young person in your group a living message to be shared with others. Like many non-Christian adults, non-Christian youth may not listen to a theological argument or doctrinal defense of the faith. But most will be attracted to the sincere words of a friend about how he or she found the Truth in a world filled with lies. They want to hear the difference God has made in *their* lives, not in someone else's. D.T. Niles has described the privilege of sharing one's faith as "one beggar telling another beggar where to get bread." Charles Swindoll described the situation in this manner:

One of the most convincing, unanswerable arguments on earth regarding Christianity is one's personal experience with the Lord Jesus Christ. No persuasive technique will ever take the place of your personal testimony. I challenge you to give serious consideration to thinking through and then presenting the way God saved you—along with the exciting results of His presence in your life.[5]

Let's accept Swindoll's challenge to help our students develop their own testimonies as they learn the importance of sharing the hope that is within them.

3. HELP STUDENTS DEVELOP THEIR OWN PERSONAL TESTIMONIES

Church youth may be a little fuzzy when asked to think through the specifics of their conversion to Christ. Most have experienced a confirmation of their faith, so to speak, as they eventually accepted ownership in later years of that which they were taught as children. Even if students are completely aware of their feelings and experiences at the time of their commitment to Christ, communicating the message to their unsaved friends can be a different matter altogether.

The Apostle Peter instructs us with these words: "But in your hearts set apart Christ as Lord. Always be prepared to give an answer to everyone who asks you to give the reason for the hope that you have" (1 Peter 3:15, NIV). The following guide will help church youth develop, write, and articulate their own personal testimonies. Several ideas for this section were adapted from *How to Make Your Mark: A Manual for Evangelism and Discipleship.*[6]

I. Develop a short, organized testimony

A. As students think through their own salvation accounts, emphasize the importance of keeping the focus on a personal commitment to Christ and what this can mean in their life.

B. Organize the presentation within a three to four minute time frame to keep it brief, to the point, and clear.

C. Help students identify their most likely audience (friends, family members, strangers) so as to gear their illustrations and points in the right direction. Relevance to one's listeners is always important in communicating the message.

II. Write it out

Give students three sheets of paper to begin writing down the specifics of their personal testimonies. Each sheet should correspond to one of the three main aspects below.

A. Aspect #1—The Before

Don't emphasize the common question, "What was your life like *before* you knew Christ?" (Remember, most of these students have "known" Christ or have known about Him all their lives.) Instead ask, "What was your life like before you gave Christ control?" Questions to help students respond include:

1. Were you ever apathetic about your faith?
2. Did you ever use excuses like, "Christians are all hypocrites" or "It's boring and irrelevant to me"?
3. Does the phrase "going through the motions" describe your experience before being committed to Christ?
4. Was your spiritual life like a roller coaster ride: up, down, and going in circles?
5. Did you have peace and an understanding about your relationship to God even before you really started living for Him?

B. Aspect #2—The Decision

1. What led to your decision to trust Christ?
2. Can you remember the occasion when you made the decision to trust Christ or made a public confession of your faith?
3. At what point did you let Christ begin to control your life?
4. Whose life influenced you most in making a decision for Christ?
5. What was your first encounter with dynamic Christianity?
6. What is your theological understanding of what Christ did for you on the cross that made your salvation possible? (This is an important point for students to be very clear on.)

C. Aspect #3—The After

1. After you gave your life to Christ, what changes took place?
2. If you trusted Christ at an early age, what happened

after you yielded control of your life to Him as Lord? What specific changes did you experience (e.g., peace, hope, joy, self-control, change in actions, new attitudes)? Encourage students to be specific and illustrative here.

3. What does Jesus Christ mean to you now?
As students think about this question, have them imagine non-Christian friends asking them what Christ means to them. Encourage your young people to be as descriptive as possible, using relevant examples.

D. Other Suggestions
1. After students have filled out their three sheets, have them condense their responses to a one-page outline.
2. Make sure the material used is accurate, concise, relevant, and illustrative, focused on a personal commitment to Christ.
3. Have volunteer adult leaders review written testimonies with students, working with them to condense the one-page outline to a 3″ x 5″ card.

III. Articulate the testimony

A. Memorization
1. Instruct students to read their cards, then practice until they can talk naturally without notes.
2. Challenge students to practice with family or friends, reminding them to keep their testimonies to three or four minutes.

B. Format
1. Begin with an attention-getting sentence or incident. Avoid starting a testimony with statements such as, "I was raised in a Christian home" or "I became a Christian when I was nine." Doing so tends to alienate non-Christians. Instead, share an experience, feeling, or attitude unbelievers can understand.
2. Avoid using Christian jargon, buzz-words, and clichés. Normal English and simple terminology usually work best. When using biblical words such as sin, born again, or eternal life, be sure to explain their meanings.
3. Conclude by relating a specific change in behavior or attitude that Christ has made.

C. Do's and Don'ts

1. Do	2. Don't
a. Be clear and concise	a. Be vague
b. Be enthusiastic	b. Be canned
c. Be interesting	c. Be boring
d. Be positive	d. Be negative
e. Be personal	e. Act like a professional
f. Be relaxed	f. Be nervous
g. Be conversational	g. Preach
h. Be persuasive	h. Argue
i. Be truthful	i. Embellish

ENERGIZING FOR EVANGELISM

As stated in the opening chapter, sometimes getting church youth to share their faith can be as tough as trying to pull teeth from a hungry alligator! It *can* be a challenge, but when given the right encouragement, along with a couple of practical "tools" for success, teens *can* be motivated to reach out to their unsaved friends. Here are several suggestions to consider.

1. SENSITIZE TO ENERGIZE

David Veerman, former National Campus Life Director for Youth for Christ/USA noted in his book *Youth Evangelism,* "The first step in mobilizing young people for effective communication of the Gospel is to help them realize that their friends are lost in their sins, unfulfilled, hopeless, and hell-bound without Christ."[7]

Veerman went on to state that the majority of youth, especially junior highers (but also senior highers), lack the understanding that their unsaved friends are truly lost. And they seldom seriously consider the consequences of their friends' unregenerate states.

It is important, therefore, that youth workers continually sensitize their students to the spiritual bankruptcy of their unsaved friends and challenge them to be assertive in sharing their faith. Mention this situation in your youth meetings through talks, small group discussions, etc. A week should not go by without encouraging your teens to share the good news of their salvation in Christ with at least one friend who needs to hear. As one youth worker put it, "Witnessing is introducing our friend on earth to our Friend in heaven."[8]

One way your students can begin sharing their faith is through the use of tracts. Campus Crusade for Christ's *Four Spiritual Laws*, written by the founder, Bill Bright, is perhaps the best known and has been successfully used by literally millions. I've found students particularly enthusiastic in using Youth for Christ's tract, *Your Most Important Relationship*. This pocket-sized tract not only presents the ideas of man, sin, the cross, and eternal life in an easy-to-understand manner, it is also visually complemented with contemporary illustrations and graphics.

An evangelism tool that I've personally used with much success and that I also "arm" my volunteer staff and students with is the tried and tested Romans Road. This tool is a vehicle for presenting the Gospel by means of a scriptural path through the Book of Romans. Church youth enjoy this particular method because it gives them some hands-on ammunition straight from the Bible. It provides a clear presentation of salvation when combined with a student's personal testimony. Here's how it works:

First, have students open their Bibles to the Book of Romans and pencil in Romans 3:10 somewhere on the title page. When the opportunity arises to share the Gospel with an unsaved friend, they simply turn to that page and will know where to begin. Romans 3:10 reads, "As it is written, 'There is none righteous, not even one.' " This passage alerts the unsaved to their state of sin.

Next to Romans 3:10 students should write Romans 3:23, which is the next cue. The "road" continues on to confront an individual with their need for God and an understanding of what God has done through Christ Jesus on the cross. The Scriptures that follow Romans 3:23 in order are: Romans 5:12; 6:23; 5:8; and 10:9-10. Following the Romans Road through these verses ultimately leads to an opportunity to invite the inquirer to trust in Christ as his or her personal Savior.

There are, of course, other tools and methods that can be used. You might already be using a different one to equip your students with the Gospel. That's fine. The important thing is to provide students with something they can effectively use when the opportunity presents itself. G. Michael Cocoris illustrates the value of a strategic approach—whatever one you choose—with this story: "A lady once told an evangelist, 'I don't like your method.' He replied, 'I'm not totally satisfied with it myself. What's yours?' She answered, 'I don't have one,' to which the evangelist responded, 'I like my method better than yours.' "[9]

2. TAKE STUDENTS WITH YOU

Experience is the best teacher—especially when attempting to energize church youth to evangelize. Youth minister John Musselman summarized this need for experience, "Part of the evangelism training for youth includes classroom instruction. But it's not enough to hold classes on witnessing. Youth must be *shown* how to witness. They should learn by observing an experienced person evangelizing someone else."[10]

I'm a living testimony to the truth of these statements. When I was a junior in high school, my youth minister asked me to go with him on a call. That night I observed Rick lead a person to Christ. I had heard lots of talks on witnessing, but seeing it done in person greatly impacted me. That one experience motivated me to share my faith with my unsaved friends more than all the talks I heard on evangelism combined.

As a youth worker, you need to make the most of every evangelistic opportunity that comes along. And when you do, be sure to take a student with you. You'll be glad you did!

3. PROGRAM FOR OUTREACH POTENTIAL

Most youth groups provide a variety of different ministries for their students. To stimulate discipleship, growth, and spiritual maturity, such opportunities as small group involvement, Sunday School, group leadership, and service are certainly appropriate. But what about opportunities for outreach? Many teens don't feel comfortable bringing their friends to a serious Bible study or prayer time. Although these more spiritually oriented meetings can in fact challenge non-Christians, it is also essential to provide nonthreatening programs and activities that unbelievers would feel comfortable attending.

One idea is a lively midweek student gathering filled with high energy music, media, and practical topics of a spiritual nature that might appeal to non-Christian teens. This type of programming is being used by youth groups across the nation because many youth workers have found that it promotes outreach among church youth. When youth workers plan events with creative programming to which their students may invite their friends, they both assist and encourage the evangelistic process.

Other nonthreatening, "come and see" activities and programming ideas include,

- concerts
- special speakers, such as athletes or celebrities
- car rallies
- broom hockey at a local ice rink
- talent shows
- air band or lip-sync competitions
- dances (check with your church leadership first)
- rallies and parties after school games
- beach trips, pool parties, lake days
- gym nights
- scavenger hunts
- movie nights

I realize that not all of these activities are suited for pulling out the *Four Spiritual Laws*, but they will give your students opportunities to get their friends' feet in the door of your group. And remember, we don't need to "candy coat" the Gospel to make it palatable for unbelievers. The majority of students coming to a church youth group activity expect some kind of spiritual emphasis. Our job is simply to introduce them to salvation through Jesus Christ. And after that—who knows how the Holy Spirit may work?

THINK ABOUT IT

1. Reflect on your own conversion experience. How would you describe it? Check the appropriate responses.
   - ☐ Average, no thrills   ☐ Black-and-white change
   - ☐ Grew up in the church   ☐ Excited to share about it
   - ☐ Radical salvation   ☐ Unmotivated to share about it

2. What have you done in your ministry to make your students think about their testimonies—positive (e.g., sharing them, writing them out), or negative (e.g., opportunities for comparison)? What positive things can you do in the future?

3. God uses many different kinds of situations to bring people into the kingdom. Think of several young people in your current group who have come to the Lord in completely different ways.

4. How does your group respond to personal evangelism? Circle the best response.

(a) unsure (b) apathetic (c) aggressive (d) enthusiastic
but unprepared

How can you better prepare them to witness?

5. List the nonthreatening activities you provide in your program that encourage students to bring their unsaved friends. Do students come in contact with the Gospel at these events?

6. Pray that your students will develop hearts for sharing their faith and personal testimonies with their unsaved friends. Pray also that any barriers to effective evangelism your young people face might begin to be torn down.

NOTES

1. Lyman Coleman and Denny Rydberg, *All the Way: On Discipleship*, Leader's Guide (Littleton, Colorado, Serendipity Press, 1982), pp. 45–46.
2. Joseph C. Aldrich, *Gentle Persuasion* (Portland, Oregon: Multnomah Press, 1988), p. 10.
3. Andrés Tapia, ed., *Campus Evangelism Handbook* (Downers Grove, Illinois: InterVarsity Press, 1987), p. 36.
4. Paul Lee Tan, *Encyclopedia of 7,700 Illustrations* (Rockville, Maryland: Assurance Publishers, 1979), p. 279.
5. Charles R. Swindoll, *Come Before Winter and . . . Share My Hope* (Wheaton, Illinois: Tyndale House Publishers, 1985), p. 59.
6. Campus Crusade for Christ, eds., *How to Make Your Mark: A Manual for Evangelism and Discipleship* (San Bernardino, California: Here's Life Publishers, 1983), pp. 114–119.
7. David Veerman, *Youth Evangelism* (Wheaton, Illinois: Victor Books, 1988), p. 187.
8. Ibid., p. 191.
9. G. Michael Cocoris, *Evangelism: A Biblical Approach* (Chicago: Moody Press, 1984), p. 147.
10. John Musselman, "Training Youth for Evangelism," in *Working with Youth*, comp. Ray Willey (Wheaton, Illinois: Victor Books, 1982), p. 64.

CHAPTER SIX

COPING WITH QUESTIONS, DEALING WITH DOUBT

The scene is a courtroom. On trial: the validity of the Christian faith—its teachings, claims, and practices.

You, Joe or Jane youth worker, are the defendant going up against a most formidable opponent.

The prosecution: Charlie church kid. A 17-year veteran of the Sunday School department. And he's got some serious ammunition of questions and doubts ready to hurl your way.

PROSECUTION: Isn't it true that our God is supposed to be a God of love? If so, then explain to me why He allows innocent children to suffer.

DEFENSE:	That's a very insightful question. Let's see. . . .
PROSECUTION:	And what about all the different denominations within Christianity? How can they all be correct? Don't such divisions prove there is no true unity in the Christian faith?
DEFENSE:	Just because there are divisions within the Christian church doesn't mean that's the way God intended it.
PROSECUTION:	Tell me something I don't know! Which brings me to my next question: How do we know the Bible is completely reliable?
DEFENSE:	Are you questioning the authority of Scripture?
PROSECUTION:	I'm asking the questions here if you don't mind.
DEFENSE:	Indeed.
PROSECUTION:	If Christianity really works, then how come there are so many hypocrites? Take my parents for example.
DEFENSE:	You're not responsible for their actions.
PROSECUTION:	Not good enough.
DEFENSE:	I'm sorry.
PROSECUTION:	(Pause) So am I. . . .

After years of growing up in a Christian environment, there likely will come a time when a young person questions the faith he or she has known for so long. This usually happens during the junior or senior years of high school.

I remember as a junior leading the charge of the local Doubters Anonymous club in my youth group. We tackled any and all subjects dealing with theology, the world, and our faith. We were on a quest for the "real" truth. We somehow reasoned that the full story wasn't given to us in Sunday School for all those years, and we were ready for some answers.

Fortunately for us, we had a group of patient adult volunteer youth workers who helped us grow through this time. They didn't argue with us or put us down for our concerns, but encouraged us to search the Scriptures and dialogue with them as we pursued our questions.

Fielding questions and doubts is never an easy task. Some students will be more honest and well-intentioned in their doubts than others. Youth workers may view doubts and questions as a lack of faith, wondering if there is a serious spiritual problem at the root of such concerns. Others may disregard the adolescent's search as an unimportant and passing phase. Still others might worry that they've said or taught something that has caused their students to doubt. It is easy as youth workers to become suspicious of questioning students and be threatened by our own inability to provide answers. Whether you're struggling or not with this particular area in your ministry, relax. I invite you to consider some of the following issues in dealing with the dilemma of doubt.

DON'T PANIC, IT'S NORMAL

Adolescence is typically a time of challenging and questioning — whether it be the authority of a parent, words of a teacher, or advice of a friend. Studies in faith development suggest that it is absolutely normal for older teens to grapple with the validity of their faith.

A study by John Westerhoff III demonstrated that faith develops in connection with the mind, will, and emotions as it progresses from a "foundational" to an "owned" stage in the life of the believer. Westerhoff described the period of late adolescence as the stage of "searching faith." Searching faith . . . move[s] from an understanding of faith that belongs to the community to an understanding of faith that is our own, we need to doubt and question that faith. At this point the 'religion of the head' becomes equally important with the 'religion of the heart.' "[1]

Perhaps you have some students who are going through this "searching" stage in your group — young people who are trying to discover deeper meaning and application for a faith they have taken at face value for so long. Teens moving into advanced stages of adolescent development begin thinking conceptually about their faith. Instead of asking the what, where, and who questions which characterized earlier faith discoveries, these teens are asking why and how questions.

Craig was a senior in high school searching for answers that involved the modern charismatic movement. Not coming from that particular tradition, he wanted to know why some Christians spoke in tongues and seemed to experience miraculous healings and others did not. Craig wanted to understand about prophecies, words of knowledge, and the laying on of hands and why his church didn't practice such customs, even when the Bible spoke of them. These questions were necessary for Craig to address as he came to understand and later defend the traditions of his own Christian heritage and background. He also learned to appreciate the practices of his other Christian friends.

Doubts and questions can also be considered normal because they come at a time when young people begin to move toward independence. There's something about getting a driver's license, a part-time job, and a girlfriend/boyfriend that changes teens. Suddenly they want to be treated more like adults. As youth learn to appreciate their privileges and handle added responsibilities, they slowly mature and strive for greater independence.

Don't be surprised when that desire for independence manifests itself in the area of a teen's faith. Like Craig, some will begin to question the established traditions of their particular Christian upbringing. Everything from church doctrine and polity to individual morality and conscience will suddenly become issues for contention. Hang in there with these students!

Just as it is normal to expect a young man or woman to grow in independence socially, likewise it is normal for him or her to do so spiritually.

So relax. It's OK if some of your students are wondering whether God really knows what He's doing. It's normal. God welcomes their search. John Fischer wrote, "Finding is no more the end of seeking than faith is the end of doubt or forgiveness the end of sin."[2]

The time to worry is when your students *don't* have any questions or concerns in regard to their faith. Don't be deceived by the loyal and faithful who give a hearty "amen" to everything told them. Spiritual apathy and complacency can set in all too easily. I like Frederick Buechner's advice when he assures us, "Doubts are the ants in the pants of faith. They keep it awake and moving."[3]

A STRENGTHENED FAITH

Can having doubts about the Christian faith really be a healthy thing for young believers? Don't the waves of doubt rock the boat of basic belief and biblical truth? Aren't doubts about God or the Christian life just plain wrong?

Not necessarily.

There is a kind of doubt that is honest and sincere. It compels young Christians to linger after a youth meeting has ended for further investigation and discussion. It reads between the lines and scrutinizes the fine print. It is doubting in the truest sense of the word. To quote Verne Becker, "True doubters are special people, people not satisfied with simplistic answers to complicated questions."[4]

You may have students who doubt. Be encouraged. For in their search for truth, faith is strengthened. In their thirst for knowledge, understanding is gained. In their quest for spiritual insight, God becomes more fully known.

There are, however, important truths the Bible speaks clearly about that need not be doubted. Forgiveness of sin, the gift of the Holy Spirit, and the promise of eternal life are foundational elements to a Christian's belief system that must be clearly understood.

Yet there are many issues where Scripture does not give black-and-white answers. Exploration is needed. Church youth must learn to dig deep to gain understanding in more complex matters of the faith. So avoid making the mistake of squelching and denying your young people opportunities to ask the tough questions. Refrain from responding with automatic proof texts and clichés. Fischer observed the damage these actions can do.

> So we bring up our children to acknowledge the answer and close the door on any questions. The end result of this kind of thinking is a narrowing of truth and experience. "Jesus is the answer" for many has turned into a restriction rather than a freedom. Like the Swami character Johnny Carson plays on late night television, Christians hold the envelope up to their heads, close their eyes, and utter the answer: Jesus. No matter what the question is, the answer will always be the same. The question becomes irrelevant. Soon, questioning in general becomes a rigid, tight, closed system where the question is viewed as a threat or the evidence of unbelief or lack of faith.[5]

Because Jesus *is* the answer, we can confidently ask the questions. Following are the most common areas of concern church youth struggle with. It is by no means an exhaustive list. My purpose in mentioning these issues is to help you prepare for the confrontations when they come and to encourage you to explore them further with your own young people. I don't hope to answer these difficult questions here; I'm sure you know that volumes could and have been written on each one. However, even if you've only been in youth work a short time, I know you've already had the opportunity to discuss most of these issues.

1. SOCIAL CONCERNS

Jesus ministered to both the physical and spiritual needs of those He came in contact with. He healed the sick, fed the hungry, and defended the poor. Christ modeled for us not only the importance of bringing salvation to those who are spiritually lost but also assistance to those who are physically or socially in need.

But the needs and problems society faces are so complex the question often arises: How can Christianity really make a difference? Students see that there is hunger in the world, yet they know Christians with overweight dogs. They also see human suffering at the hands of disease, natural disaster, crime, poverty, and inhumane governments.

They hear of people beaten and killed because their skin happens to be a different color than someone else's. They see war continue to rob their planet of peace, country against country and faith against faith. Immorality, materialism, and their many consequences are rampant, while the homeless still line our streets.

It is these situations and problems that may drive students to cry out, "Where is God in all of this?" "Does He know what's going on?" "Does He care?" "Why don't more Christians get involved?" "How can I believe in a God who can allow all this to happen?" Tough questions—and no easy answers.

2. OTHER RELIGIONS

Church youth may be shocked when they first encounter the beliefs and practices of other religions. Most feel nervous and unsure enough when called upon to defend their own faith in a logical manner, much less refute the theology or practices of a non-Christian religion or a different denomination!

On several occasions I've had students phone me after talking with a Mormon at school. Questions concerning Christology, the Trinity, eternal life, and salvation all come up. Students realize that they might not be prepared to challenge the beliefs of others until they've really thought through their own. Talk about a teachable moment!

3. PERSONAL FAITH

Doubts are almost a prerequisite for developing a stronger and more mature faith. Consider the analogy of a growing child. Babies at first require food that is easily digestible and doesn't have to be chewed. As they grow and develop teeth, they are ready for solid food that must be chewed.

In the same way, church youth might first be introduced to spiritual food in the form of flannelgraph Bible stories that are easily tasted and swallowed in the Sunday School department. As they grow and mature in their Christian faith, their spiritual eating habits change. They progress to the "meat" of the Word and learn to chew the food of their faith awhile before digesting it completely.

The issue of *feelings* is often chewed by doubting youth as they ask themselves questions like these: How come I don't *feel* like praying, reading my Bible, or serving others? If I don't *feel like a* Christian, is something wrong? Students may also have doubts concerning the *Bible:* How can I know for sure the Scriptures are reliable? Do science and theology contradict each other? Does God use miracles today?

Seemingly *unanswered prayer* can also be an area of concern. The struggle for *personal holiness* in the life of a blooming young believer can sometimes cause conflict. Questions and problems such as these arise: If God forgives my sins, why do I still feel so guilty? I pray to avoid temptation, but I always seem to fall into it. It isn't fair! If Christianity is true, then why are there so many hypocrites?

Finally, a teen's *church background* can also become an issue. How do I know my particular church tradition is the right one? Does it even matter? Is my church really biblical in its teaching, approach, and practices?

With the right guidance and encouragement, church youth will grow in their faith as they chew on these questions and doubts. Your job is to help bring them through as you explore the answers together.

A WEAKENED FAITH

In 1870, Hannah Whitall Smith wrote her classic devotional, *The Christian's Secret of a Happy Life.* She considered doubt a major stumbling block for Christians of her day.

It seems strange that people whose very name of Believers implies that their one chiefest characteristic is that they believe, should have to confess that they have doubts. And yet it is such a universal habit, that I feel, if the name were to be given over again, the only fitting and descriptive name that could be given to many of God's children would have to be that of Doubters.[6]

Doubters rather than believers—there may be truth to that statement. But in context, Mrs. Smith's concern was not with the doubts themselves but with what Christians *do* with them. Some, as we discussed, become stronger Christians as a result of working through their questions and doubts. Others, however, allow doubt to weaken their faith or use it as an excuse for an already struggling faith.

In working with church youth, I've found that the *attitude* a student has regarding his doubts and questions determines the spiritual response he or she will have. Consider some of the following doubt factors that contribute to a weakened faith:

"DON'T GIVE ME ANSWERS; I JUST WANT AN ARGUMENT"

The Pharisees were religious to the core, the ultra-pious of Christ's day. They were respected teachers and considered the guardians of the Jewish faith. The average Jewish person marveled at their acts of piety and personal sacrifice. From lying prostrate in the streets for prayer to their sunken and pale faces from fasting to their copious leadership at the holy feasts, these men were the picture of upright religiosity. But they had a sincerity problem.

While the masses stood in awe of these leaders, Jesus saw through their false piety to their insincere hearts. On several occasions, the Pharisees tried to trap Jesus with questions. They questioned Him regarding His authority (Matthew 21:23-27), challenged His loyalties to God and the Roman government (Matthew 22:15-22), and tested His knowledge and understanding of the law (Matthew 22:34-40). Were these pious men seeking the truth? No. Jesus discerned that their intent was not to find real answers but to undermine His following and thereby destroy His threat to their leadership. In response to the Pharisees' inquiries, Jesus typically turned the questions back on them to reveal their own hypocrisy.

To be sure, church youth can grow and mature spiritually as they work through their doubts, but doubting out of insincerity or for argument's sake can only lead to a type of Pharisaism. Like the Pharisees, a false sense of pride or extreme need for attention commonly lies at the root of such destructive attitudes.

Steve liked to play the big shot. He looked forward to questioning everything I said or taught in the youth group. During my talks, while most of the students were trying to pay attention and learn, Steve was looking for any and every issue he thought might "put me on the spot." It wasn't that Steve was an atheist; I believe he truly loved the Lord. He had a problem with pride (like the Pharisees) and used doubt and questioning as vehicles for gaining a false sense of superiority. I talked with Steve, and together we discovered that his doubts and questions were based on a prideful and insincere attitude. By dealing with deeper issues, Steve was able to realize how his actions were hurting, rather than helping, his relationship with the Lord and others.

"I DON'T WANT TO BE COMMITTED"

Doubts can also arise during times of spiritual stagnation and lack of commitment. Commitment and belief are two concepts that naturally complement each other. To be committed to something or someone implies a certain amount of belief. For example, an athlete who believes in his abilities will be committed to training if he wants to improve and succeed in his given sport. If he isn't committed to training, his performance is bound to reflect it. If the athlete continues to approach his sport in an uncommitted fashion, soon he will begin to doubt himself, his ability, and his intent.

A few years back, I was on a church softball team. We were all pretty good athletes and decided we would forego practicing and just show up at the games. We figured that we'd do all right as long as at least nine of us took the field. We were wrong. Week after week we were beaten by teams who were committed to slow-pitch softball. (They even practiced once a week!) By midseason, it was clear that our lack of commitment had become the demise of our team. If someone would have walked up to me or any member of the team before a game and asked if we were going to win, the response would have likely been a lackluster, "I doubt it."

Just as belief and commitment go hand in hand, doubts and lack of commitment are also related. Show me a kid who has been slacking off in his commitment to Christ, and I'll show you a kid who's doubting whether Christianity is really all it professes to be.

As a youth worker, it pays to observe uncommitted students closely. Some may verbalize their doubts and frustrations while others silently and painfully internalize theirs.

When counseling students who are struggling with doubts and questions, ask the penetrating questions and observe the outward signs. Is there unconfessed sin? What about neglect of prayer and time spent in God's Word or absence from youth group meetings and church services?

Helping coach a student back into contact with Christ and His body will help to rebuild weakened spiritual muscles. Before too long, a student's reasons for doubts will turn into opportunities for faith. As the writer to the Hebrews admonished, "Therefore, since we have so great a cloud of witnesses surrounding us, let us also lay aside every encumbrance, and the sin which so easily entangles us, and let us run with endurance the race that is set before us, fixing our eyes on Jesus, the author and perfecter of faith" (Hebrews 12:1-2).

In light of a growing relationship with Christ, many questions may become insignificant indeed.

"I DOUBT; THEREFORE I REBEL"

Sometimes teens use doubts as smoke screens to justify their rebellious attitudes and actions. As they try to rationalize a disobedient lifestyle, they may use doubt as an excuse. For example, they might say, "All Christians are phonies anyway; the Christian life doesn't really work," in hopes of justifying their own hypocrisy. Or some might add, "The Bible can't conclusively prove God exists; you have to take it on faith. Well, I can't anymore!" Statements such as these are often used as defense mechanisms to make the rebellious Christian teenager feel better about his own disobedience, no matter what form it takes.

Again, let me stress it is not the doubts themselves that weaken faith, but the harmful and belligerent attitude with which they are expressed. The intent for spiritual growth through this person's doubts is completely missing. When wayward Christian young people use doubts as façades for disobedience and rebellion, their attitudes and actions must be confronted immediately. If ignored, the negative spirit with which their doubts are raised might not only ruin their faith, but lead others in the group astray as well.

DEALING WITH DOUBTERS

Perhaps after reading this chapter you're beginning to have some doubts of your own—whether you're really up for the challenge of dealing with the doubters in your group! Have faith. There are several ways to minister and encourage students who are dabbling with doubt.

First, make it a general practice to provide a nonthreatening atmosphere in your group where doubts and questions are welcomed, rather than discouraged. Encourage students to ask, seek, and knock as they learn to explore the deeper issues of their faith. The Scriptures don't always provide black-and-white answers to all of life's tough questions.

As a youth worker, remember to not give simple answers too readily. Rather, challenge students to think new thoughts about old issues and struggle through the complexities of their faith. Enlighten them to the fact that faith itself is a bit of a mystery, "the assurance of things hoped for, the conviction of things not seen" (Hebrews 11:1).

Second, let them know that as doubters, they are in good company. In the Book of Job alone, there are 288 unanswered questions posed by the man from Uz and his friends. David (the man after God's own heart) and his son, Solomon (the Bible's wisest man), each had doubts and questions about God (Psalm 13; 22:1-2; Ecclesiastes 1:2, 13-14). In the New Testament there were doubters too. John the Baptist wondered if Jesus was the promised Messiah (Matthew 11:2-6), and the Apostle Thomas doubted whether Jesus really rose from the dead (John 20:24-29).

Third, you may wish to provide a separate study group for students interested in digging deeper into God's Word. Teach them to be like the first-century Bereans who "received the word with great eagerness, examining the Scriptures daily, to see whether these things [the teachings of Paul and Silas] were so" (Acts 17:11). You may also choose to go through a book dealing with questions about the Christian faith, such as *Answers to Tough Questions Skeptics Ask about the Christian Faith* by Josh McDowell and Don Stewart, *The Sunnier Side of Doubt* by Allister E. McGrath, or *Questions? Answers!* by Verne Becker, Tim Stafford, and Philip Yancey. There are also excellent books dealing with theological issues, ethics, social issues, and the Christian life in general. Most important, don't allow students to stay bogged down in the questions, but help them make progress toward understanding.

Fourth, become sensitive to the spirit and attitude with which your students raise questions and doubts. Determine if a negative underlying cause is fueling a student's doubts. Some may be struggling with issues about God or the Christian life in such a way that their faith is weakened. James 1:6 warns, "For the one who doubts is like the surf of the sea driven and tossed by the wind." Teens need an anchor to hold onto. Give them personal support, guidance, and love, grounded in the hope and assurance of their salvation in Christ Jesus.

Finally, remind students of the words of Walt Allmand, "Doubt your doubts before you doubt your beliefs." While doubts are normal and understood by God, it is crucial that they not become the focus of our faith. Rather, let us focus on our faith and grow through our doubts.

THINK ABOUT IT

1. What is your initial reaction when students express doubts about their faith?

2. What were some of the doubts and questions you had as a Christian teenager? If you weren't a Christian in your teen years, were there specific issues that stood in your way?

3. List some of the more difficult issues your students are dealing with in terms of their Christian faith. How might you begin to address these issues corporately? Individually?

4. Offer a Doubters Anonymous club for your students. Meet with them weekly, biweekly, or monthly to discuss their questions, doubts, concerns, and issues. What steps do you need to take to get started?

5. Think of several students in your group who might be spiritually weakened as a result of their doubts. Make appointments with each of them in the next few weeks them to confront, encourage, and/or assure them.

NOTES

1. John H. Westerhoff III, *Will Our Children Have Faith?* (New York: Seabury Press, 1976), pp. 96.
2. John Fischer, *True Believers Don't Ask Why* (Minneapolis: Bethany House Publishers, 1989), p. 71.
3. Frederick Buechner, *Wishful Thinking: A Theological ABC* (New York: Harper & Row Publishers, 1973), p. 20.
4. Verne Becker, Tim Stafford, and Philip Yancey, *Questions? Answers!* (Wheaton, Illinois: Tyndale House Publishers, 1986), p. 11.
5. Fischer, p. 74.
6. Hannah Whitall Smith, *The Christian's Secret of a Happy Life* (Westwood, New Jersey: Fleming H. Revell Co., 1952), p. 106.

PLAYING WITH SIN

In California's Yosemite National Park, there are many beautiful waterfalls; but one has special meaning for me—Nevada Falls. If you hike to the top of this magnificent waterfall, you'll notice a sign that is sure to grab your attention. In big, bold letters it reads: DANGER.

A picture on the sign of someone falling over the edge leaves little doubt about exactly what kind of danger the sign is describing. The message is clear and simple: Play around with this waterfall, and you'll get hurt—even killed.

Why is it, then, that every time I hike to the top of Nevada Falls, I am tempted to get dangerously close to the edge? There's a thrill and excitement in doing something you shouldn't—something you *know* is risky. Sometimes it's the curiosity of seeing what's on the other side—or over the edge. Other times it's a friend egging you on to do it—dares and all!

But you can fall.

A high school classmate of mine courted danger by getting too close to the water's edge. Tragically, he fell into the rushing water of Nevada Falls, plunging 594 feet to his death.

Waterfalls aren't things to play around with—and neither is sin.

Despite the potential consequences, the temptation to "play with sin" for the pleasure or experience is still a major struggle for many church youth. Sin has the mysterious lure of a waterfall, and Christian young people are enticed to play with the currents of temptation, only to fall over the edge.

MISSING OUT?

Committed Christian youth are often somewhat sheltered and in-experienced in the "ways of the world." This fact doesn't mean they're unaware of what's going on in the secular world, but they themselves haven't participated in its vices. Such a state of world-ly naiveté is nothing to be ashamed of. On the contrary, it is biblically sound and morally commendable.

> I urge you therefore, brethren, by the mercies of God, to present your bodies a living and holy sacrifice, acceptable to God, which is your spiritual service of worship. And do not be conformed to this world, but be transformed by the renewing of your mind, that you may prove what the will of God is, that which is good and accept-able and perfect.
>
> (Romans 12:1-2)

As a high schooler, I was pressured Monday through Friday to "conform" to the world by my friends at school. On Wednesday nights and Sunday mornings, I was encouraged to be "trans-formed" into the image of Christ by my youth minister. What a struggle! Although I knew what was right, my sin nature did every-thing it could to get me to conform to the world's standards. I saw my friends (both Christian and unbelieving) having a great time with what I considered to be sin, and I longed to be a part of it.

However, my conscience wouldn't let me. I was held captive by what I felt at the time was the ball and chain of the Bible.

Lori was a student of mine who struggled in this same area. She had been a Christian most of her life. Recently, however, Lori was feeling "out of it" at school because a certain group of her friends were partying and she wasn't. They told her what a great time she was missing—drinking, being with guys, that sort of thing. Her friends often invited her to join them.

"I'm always missing out on the fun," Lori complained. "I want to go to the next party with my girlfriends—just to see what it's like and to experience it all once. I'll confess to God and He'll forgive me. I'll never do it again after that. I promise."

Maybe you have kids like Lori in your group—kids who are tired of being good all the time, who are ready for a little sex, drugs, and rock 'n roll. Not that they are really seeking a life of debauchery, but they are wondering what it's like. This type of reasoning is fundamentally wrong. Jerry Bridges cautions,

> In the deceitfulness of our hearts, we sometimes play with temptation by entertaining the thought that we can always confess and later ask forgiveness. Such thinking is exceedingly dangerous. God's judgment is without partiality. He never overlooks our sin. He never decides not to bother, since the sin is only a small one. No, God hates sin intensely whenever and wherever He finds it.[1]

Sadly, these excuses and rationalizations are used too often by church youth as they begin to flirt with temptation. Like the waterfall's edge, look out! Experiences don't always turn out the way we intend them to. Still, some church youth will play with sin—a game with no winners in the end.

JUMPING IN

PEER PRESSURE

I've already alluded to the fact that the pressure to conform is a major influence on church youth, one that causes many of them to compromise their Christian lifestyle. Dr. James Dobson has noted, "The word 'conformity' refers to the desire to be just like everyone else—to do what they do and say what they say, to think what they think and wear what they wear. A conformist is someone who is afraid to be different from the majority; he feels a great need to be like everyone else."[2]

The desire to be socially accepted by one's peers is a need young people keenly feel. Perhaps Christian teens feel it even more. Why? Because Christian youth *know* they're different and perhaps fear the greater risk of the crowd's ridicule or rejection. Some have the courage and integrity to stand alone when pressured, others do not.

Many students respond more to the need to be accepted by their peers than to the importance of obeying God's Word. We hear them say, "Everybody's doing it" and "It's no big deal" as they begin to rationalize the behavior they're contemplating. For example, they often take a drink or attend an R-rated movie in order to save face in front of the crowd. The pressure to conform to the world's standards is tremendous.

There are, of course, consequences. First, a teen may begin to build his or her self-esteem on the approval of others, rather than in the love of Christ. Second, by giving sin opportunities through peer pressure in adolescence, a pattern is established that can continue into Christian adulthood.

When I was in high school, I went to virtually any movie my friends wanted to see. Most of those movies compromised my Christian integrity with foul language and scenes depicting sexual immorality and violence. With that pattern established, it shouldn't be a shock that I've struggled at times with the movies I watch as an adult. "It's no big deal," I'll tell myself when a group of friends (often Christians, I might add) want to go see some award-winning film although it contains terrible language and acts of immorality.

By making allowances for our students to "play with sin," we contribute to a pattern of compromise that will plague them into adulthood. The excuses "kids will be kids" or "they just aren't 'there' yet" fall short when held up to God's standard of holiness. First Peter 1:15-16 reminds us, "But like the Holy One who called you, be holy yourselves also in all your behavior; because it is written, 'You shall be holy, for I am holy.' "

CURIOSITY

While some Christian teens drift toward the waterfall's edge as a result of the pressures of the crowd, others get too close because of curiosity. Lori, mentioned previously, fits into this category. Thoughts like these fill the minds of inquiring church youth:

- "I wonder what a party is really like."
- "I wonder what it feels like to be drunk or high."
- "I wonder what it would be like to steal something and not get caught."
- "I wonder what it's like to see an X-rated movie."
- "I wonder what having sex is like."

If allowed to develop further, this curiosity often leads to temptation . . . then to experimentation . . . resulting in sin. Admonish your students to realize that when curiosity comes knocking, they should *NOT answer the door!* Jay Kesler says, "Christians who get involved in sin are miserable. They've closed the door on sin and then spend their lives looking [back] through the keyhole."[3]

Popular Christian artist Amy Grant recorded a song a few years ago that deals with letting our curious sin nature get the best of us. Appropriately, the song is entitled "Wise Up."

Got myself in this situation
I'm not sure about
Climbing in where there's temptation
Can I get back out

I never can quite find the answer
The one I want to hear
The one that justifies my action
Says the coast is clear

Something on the outside
Says to jump on in
But something on the inside
Is telling me again

Better wise up
Better think twice
Never leave room for compromise
You better wise up
Better get smart

And use your head to guard your heart
It's gonna get rough
So you better wise up

Take a look at your intentions
When you have to choose
Could it be that apprehension
Might be telling you
To back off now is better
So take your heart and run
But get your thoughts together
Before they come undone[4]

Better wise up—good advice! Admonish your students to consider the dangers of playing with temptation for curiosity's sake. As Romans 8:8-9 warns, "Those who are in the flesh cannot please God. However, you are not in the flesh but in the Spirit, if indeed the Spirit of God dwells in you."

Sin for curiosity's sake can lead to very real and unfortunate consequences. Pregnancy, drug addiction, alcoholism, emotional distress, and ruined relationships are all possibilities for those who are just "playing around." However, it's more than just the threat of these dire results. Students begin to yield themselves to the power and influence of sin rather than the power of God. And as long as sin has a hold, students can't fully experience the victory God intends for their lives.

REBELLION

The final reason some Christian adolescents play willingly with the temptations of sin is rebellion. Sometimes an overbearing and legalistic home environment will repel a teenager in the opposite direction of the faith. In these situations, youth "get back" at their parents by openly rebelling in sinful acts of disobedience as if to communicate the message, "I don't want anything to do with you or your faith, and I'll prove it!"

In another instance, a rigid church environment can cause church youth to use sin as a weapon for rebellion. Typically, churches that major in the don'ts, such as the following, fuel the fires that lead to defiance.

● Don't dress a certain way.

- Don't mingle with the opposite sex.
- Don't dance.
- Don't grow your hair long.
- Don't listen to *any* rock music.
- Don't go to movies.
- Don't play cards.
- Don't question the pastor.
- Don't cause trouble.
- Don't have fun.
- Don't act your age.
- Don't ask why.

Dr. Donald E. Sloat, author of *The Dangers of Growing Up in a Christian Home*, reflected from his own church days as a youth.

> We also were not to be "of the world," although it was never quite clear what the "world" really was. . . . Having expensive clothes and a fancy car, telling funny stories, and having a good time all seemed to be wrong somehow. The primary emphasis was on being totally dedicated to God and maintaining a serious, sober view of life. Whatever I wanted was not important. Genuine self-assertion was acceptable only if it were done on God's behalf.[5]

Still, others might play with sin as a way of communicating disappointment or frustration toward their parents or God Himself. One young man I knew began following a self-proclaimed satanic metal band to show God how mad he was at Him for the family troubles he was having at home. After several counseling sessions, we were able to talk openly about his anger and how using sin as a vehicle for rebellion against God and his parents was not the answer to his problems.

This leads to a final observation. When purposeful acts of disobedience are used to express rebellion by young people, the youth worker should look for frustration and unresolved conflict to be at the root of the problem. Ask troubled students penetrating questions that are both honest and direct. Question them as to their relationships at home, school, church, and with God. Find out what areas of conflict they haven't been able to deal with in more constructive, biblically based ways. Then help them in these areas. Rebelling in acts of sin can lead a Christian young person into deeper spiritual bankruptcy if allowed to go unchecked.

HELPING STUDENTS

Teens who have grown up in the church *know* it's wrong to play with sin. By condemning them, we may only make the situation worse. When ministering to these students, it is good to begin by appealing to the authority of God's Word. Remember, most church youth are firmly established in the teachings of Scripture and, though they may not always show it, respect its authority.

I suggest as a first step sitting down with the student and patiently confronting him or her with the Word. Explore the seriousness of sin as stated in the Bible. Have the student read aloud verses you've selected, and discuss them together. For example, I counsel students that "playing with sin" as a Christian is actually playing into Satan's hands. First Peter 5:8 says, "Be of sober spirit, be on the alert. Your adversary, the devil, prowls about like a roaring lion, seeking someone to devour." Temptation is the tool Satan uses to draw Christians away from God. Young people who are not alert to the seriousness of sin best sober up quickly!

James 4:7 provides our defense: "Submit therefore to God. Resist the devil and he will flee from you." Submitting to God's authority in obedience and holiness is crucial if church youth are to resist the temptations of the devil. As Paul instructed,

> In reference to your former manner of life, you lay aside the old self, which is being corrupted in accordance with the lusts of deceit, and that you be renewed in the spirit of your mind, and put on the new self, which in the likeness of God has been created in righteousness and holiness of the truth.
>
> (Ephesians 4:22-24)

One way to resist the devil and put on the new self is not to give the adversary opportunities to lead us astray (Ephesians 4:27). Help students identify influences in their lives that might be distracting them from their faith. In some cases, you may need to counsel students to choose a new group of friends in order to lessen opportunities for temptation through peer pressure. First Corinthians 15:33 warns, "Do not be deceived: 'Bad company corrupts good morals.' "

In addition, students need to realize that there are consequences to their actions. Proverbs 6:27-28 admonishes, "Can a man take fire in his bosom, and his clothes not be burned? Or can a man walk on hot coals, and his feet not be scorched?" Answer: No. In context, this verse specifically warns against involvement with adultery, but it also provides wise counsel for those wishing just to experience the pleasures of the flesh.

Also, help Christian youth understand that to experiment with sin for pleasure's sake, for the experience of it, because the crowd expects it of them, or for rebellion cheapens the work of grace wrought by Christ's death on the cross. It cost God the life of His only Son that our sins might be forgiven. For a Christian to take such a gift for granted is to practice what the Christian theologian and martyr Dietrich Bonhoeffer termed "cheap grace."

Finally, challenge youth to pray that God would take away their desire for sin and replace it with a hunger for righteousness. God desires the best for each of us. A life of holiness isn't easy, but as your students ask for God's help and yield themselves to the leading of the Holy Spirit, the rewards and blessings will reinforce their Christian lifestyle. Encourage them to trust in the promise of Philippians 2:13, "For it is God who is at work in you, both to will and to work for His good pleasure."

Sound simple? I know it's not. But slowly, as students begin to trust God to work in their lives, they *will* begin to experience victory over sin—one battle at a time.

THINK ABOUT IT

1. Describe in your own words the difference between a new Christian's struggle with sin and a church youth's struggle.

2. Have you ever had a student in your group like Lori? If so, how did you handle the situation? If not, how might you handle the situation?

3. Do your Christian young people realize the consequences of "playing around" with sin? What do you consider to be some of the consequences of this behavior?

4. On a scale of 1–10, how much influence does negative peer

pressure have on your church youth? Circle the number.

1 2 3 4 5 6 7 8 9 10

Low   High

5. How do your church kids view sin? Check the appropriate responses.

(a) Seriously   (d) Natural for everyone,
(b) Not so seriously   Christian or not
(c) As hurtful to God   (e) Always forgiven by God
                                  (f) A guilt trip

6. Do you emphasize personal holiness in your group? Why or why not?

7. When was the last time you praised your students for Christian growth and obedience, even amidst the temptations they face at school? Pick two kids and encourage them this week.

___

NOTES

1. Jerry Bridges, *The Pursuit of Holiness* (Colorado Springs, Colorado: Navpress, 1978), p. 33.
2. Dr. James Dobson, *Preparing for Adolescence* (Ventura, California: Regal Books, 1989), p. 41.
3. Quoted in *Alive*, S. Rickly Christian (Wheaton, Illinois: Tyndale House Publishers, 1988), p. 52.
4. Copyright © 1984 Meadowgreen Music Co./River Oaks Music Co. All rights administered by Meadowgreen Group—54 Music Sq. E., Suite 305, Nashville, TN 37203. International copyright secured. All rights reserved. Used by permission.
5. Donald E. Sloat, *The Dangers of Growing Up in a Christian Home* (Nashville, Tennessee: Thomas Nelson Publishers, 1986), p. 169.

PART
3

STRATEGIES FOR MINISTRY

Before a military officer gives the order to attack, before a football coach puts his team on the field, and before a politician begins a campaign, they all consider one thing: a strategy. Have you considered a strategy for effectively ministering to your students? Do you have a game plan to help them attain spiritual growth? If not, maybe it's time to go back to basic training. I know that at times I've had to.

So far in this book, we've looked at the issues that specifically concern youth who have grown up in the church. The strategies for ministry that are outlined in this final section are designed to help you challenge your church youth. However, as is the case with most sound principles, these programs and ideas can also be applied across the board to benefit your whole youth group.

RELATIONAL DISCIPLESHIP

Our new youth minister was 22 years old and fresh out of Bible college. He had red hair, thick glasses, and was unathletic to boot! I was an ornery church kid waiting to challenge and discourage yet another poor soul who accepted the youth ministry position at our church.

It was his first day of active duty, and I could tell our new leader was a bit nervous as he shared his vision for spiritual and numerical growth with us. While most of my peers were ready and willing to forge ahead, I remained skeptical. In commenting on something our youth minister said in his opening speech, I boldly proclaimed, "If you think you're going to grow this group to 30 kids, you're crazy!"

Undaunted by my "welcome," Rick made it a point to get to know me on a personal basis. I didn't know it at the time, but Rick had not only befriended me but began discipling me. Over the years, his example not only challenged me to grow in the Lord but ultimately motivated me to go into youth ministry.

CHARACTERISTICS

After years of working in church youth ministry, I've come to a brilliant observation: Church youth are not impressed with programs. Nothing new, right? Sure, you might get a large turnout by hosting concerts and multimedia extravaganzas once in a while, but your kids have seen programs come and go. Unfortunately, they've probably seen their fair share of youth workers come and go too, since the average youth worker stays less than two years!

It's no wonder church youth around our nation are bored with their faith and disinterested in the church. We are facing a crisis of consistency in local church youth ministry. Young people are starving for personal input, encouragement, and spiritual challenge. Who's giving it to them in *your* church?

Building strong relationships is the key to ultimately discipling Christian young people, and lasting discipleship takes time. Jesus spent no less than three years with His 12 disciples. Discipleship involves more than programs of Bible memorization, study manuals, or watching a series of spiritual videos. Lasting discipleship is the process by which Christian character is developed as one life touches another. I like the way one youth worker put it when he said, "Discipleship without relationship is a contradiction in terms."[1]

The following traits characterize a relational approach to discipleship with church youth. Whether your group is large, medium, or small, developing these traits in your life and the lives of other leaders is a must for effective student discipleship.

TRAIT #1 — AVAILABILITY
Today's lifestyle is characterized by busyness. And the life of the average youth worker is no exception. We've become a lot like the proverbial busy bee and beaver—always working to fill one more honeycomb or build one more dam. We push our energies to the limit in a frantic attempt to get more kids out to our programs,

rather than spending time with the ones we already have. We struggle to faithfully teach the Bible to our students week in and week out and become frustrated when we get a less than enthusiastic response.

Perhaps the problem lies not in the teaching of lessons but in the neglect of building meaningful relationships with kids. I like to remember the saying, "They won't care how much you know until they know how much you care."

Being available is one way to show your students that they are important to you, and it's the first step in beginning the discipleship process. The Apostle Paul exemplified the quality of availability as he ministered to the church at Thessalonica: "But we proved to be gentle among you, as a nursing mother tenderly cares for her own children. Having thus a fond affection for you, we were well-pleased to impart to you not only the Gospel of God but also our own lives, because you had become very dear to us" (1 Thessalonians 2:7-8).

For youth who have grown up in the church, the Gospel of God has already been imparted, but what about the *lives* of men and women who are willing to make themselves available to spend time with these students? Informal time with teens at the mall or local yogurt shop can give them an opportunity to open up in a way that they might not in Sunday School. Being available when students are hurting is also important in building a relationship that goes beyond the walls of the church building. Actions speak louder than words—especially when a young person is hurting. A poem by a junior higher illustrates this point clearly:

> You spoke to me of love
>   I doubted you.
> You spoke to me of caring
>   I doubted you.
> You spoke to me of self-worth
>   I doubted you still.
> You came to visit me in the hospital today
>   I believed everything you said.[2]

TRAIT #2—MODELING
For most church youth, the qualities and characteristics of the Christian life are first modeled in the home. Parents' examples

have the greatest influences on the lives of children as they begin to assimilate the Christian faith. I recall my parents quietly modeling qualities of the fruit of the Spirit when I was a child.

Dad was consistently patient and self-controlled as he dealt with all kinds of difficult situations. Mom modeled love, joy, kindness, and gentleness. Her care and concern for her family and others, both in word and in deed, has made a lasting impact on me. And while the parents of my friends were splitting up and drifting away from the Lord, Mom and Dad remained faithful both to God and to each other. Because of their example, I knew Christianity was more than attending church services on Sundays and Wednesdays; it was a relationship with God that works 24 hours a day.

But although I was raised in a Christian home, there were times of spiritual stagnation, apathy, and rebellion in my life. As a teenager, I sought role models outside my home to motivate and challenge me spiritually. Church youth need adult leaders who will not only spend time with them but who will model the Christian life in front of them on a consistent basis.

In his classic book *The Master Plan of Evangelism*, Robert E. Coleman described Jesus' method of modeling:

> Jesus had no formal school, no Seminaries, no outlined course of study, no periodic membership classes in which He enrolled His followers. None of these highly organized procedures considered so necessary today entered at all into His ministry. Amazing as it may seem, all Jesus did to teach these men His way was to draw them close to Himself. He was His own school and curriculum.[3]

Think of the lessons Jesus' disciples learned by just being with Him in the context of everyday living. For example, they learned about religious hypocrisy from the way Jesus dealt with the Pharisees and scribes (Matthew 23:1-36). They learned about concern for the sick and outcast as Jesus ministered to the masses. They learned about their own prejudice as Jesus dealt with the Samaritan woman (John 4). They learned about forgiveness as Jesus ministered to a woman caught in adultery (John 8:1-11). And they learned about devotion to God as they witnessed their master in personal prayer (Matthew 14:23).

Youth leaders also have these kinds of opportunities to model Christianity in today's laboratory of life. First, invite kids to spend time with you. Then take advantage of teachable moments. A lesson on morality can be learned in a music store, just as a thought on materialism can be shared in a local shopping mall. Whether it's on the church grounds or on the streets of the inner city, Christian modeling in everyday situations will have a great impact on the lives of your church youth.

In writing to a group of Christians in the city of Philippi, Paul said: "The things you have learned and received and heard and seen in me, practice these things; and the God of peace shall be with you" (Philippians 4:9). The Apostle Paul understood the importance and impact of being an example to others in Christian godliness and character. Wise words indeed for ministering to church youth.

TRAIT #3 — ACCOUNTABILITY
Tony Dorsett was one of the greatest running backs the National Football League has ever seen. In 1981 he became the first player to ever rush for more than 1,000 yards in each of his first five seasons. During his 11 years with the Dallas Cowboys, Dorsett gained an incredible 12,036 yards, placing him third on the all-time leading rusher's list. Of his abilities, his longtime coach Tom Landry said, "I don't know that I've ever seen a greater natural halfback than Tony Dorsett. No one could hit a hole quicker. And once he broke into the open field, his running instincts were a wonder to watch."[4]

To be sure, Dorsett was one of the greatest players of the game; but even with his superstar status, he wasn't beyond the authority of his head coach. I can still remember watching TV several years ago and hearing that Tony Dorsett had been benched for a nationally televised game because he had missed an unexcused practice. The star player's parents had even flown into Dallas for the game, but they would not witness their son play that Sunday afternoon. Tom Landry held his star player accountable not only for his actions but also for his responsibility to his teammates. What an example of accountability for those of us working with youth!

In a way, we in church youth work are coaches too, responsible for our own teams. Keeping our students accountable spiritually is a challenge we cannot afford to disregard. Just as we need to hold a new Christian accountable for laying aside the old self and putting on the new (Ephesians 4:22-24), we also need to hold veteran Christian young people accountable for being "doers of the word, and not merely hearers" (James 1:22).

Without some type of spiritual accountability in your discipling relationships, the possibility for mediocrity and stagnation exists. In speaking of the importance of spiritual accountability, Gordon MacDonald wrote,

> No one grows where truth is absent. No one is pushed *to be* and *to do* the best. And when you look at this deficit from a Christian perspective, it describes a situation where men and women are never going to become all that God has made them to be nor will they gather the spiritual energy or passion to make it happen.[5]

Reflecting on those words, I am reminded of the way Jesus dealt with His wayward disciple Peter. You'll remember that Peter was the one who denied Christ three times (Luke 22:54-62). Realizing his great sin, Peter was no doubt crushed, feeling like a disloyal friend and spiritual failure. But Jesus didn't allow failure to defeat Peter. He knew His disciple's potential and future role in establishing the church. Soon after His resurrection, Jesus held Peter accountable for his actions and reestablished His relationship with him. John 21:15-17 tells us that Peter confessed his love for his Savior three times (which was no coincidence by the way); then Jesus held His disciple accountable for feeding His sheep. By reading the Book of Acts, it's apparent that Peter heard Jesus' message loud and clear.

Church youth also need to be sensitively confronted and challenged with the truth of their lives by caring adult leaders who see their potential. I make it a practice to consistently hold students accountable for moral purity in their dating relationships, honesty and integrity at school, and thoughtfulness in their friendships with one another.

An adult leader I once worked with was great at keeping his small group of freshmen guys accountable for the music they listened to and the movies they watched. His goal was to teach his students consistency in their Christian lives outside the church environment. When one of his guys blew it, he let him know. But he also let them know how much he loved them. He practiced Proverbs 27:5-6: "Better is open rebuke than love that is concealed. Faithful are the wounds of a friend."

Finally, church youth need accountability in terms of their commitment to Christ if they are to grow and eventually attain their spiritual goals. Again, I turn to Tom Landry whose definition of coaching provides insight into this area. Landry defined coaching this way: "To get men to do what they don't want to do in order to achieve what they want to achieve."[6]

If that's not our task in church youth ministry, then I don't know what is. In other words, our job is to get students to do what they might not want to do in order to achieve what they want to achieve spiritually. You and your fellow leaders can begin holding kids accountable in such areas as:

- personal time in prayer and Bible study
- service
- involvement and attendance
- sharing their faith
- student leadership
- ministry involvement
- integrity and morality

Like coaching, motivating church youth toward personal growth and spirituality is a challenge. And although students may balk at your initial attempts, don't be discouraged. On the inside, the majority are glad that someone is interested enough in them to hold them accountable for growth in Christ.

APPROACHES

Hule Goddard and Jorge Acevedo stated in their book *The Heart of Youth Ministry*, "Relationship is the bridge over which discipleship flows. . . . Even programmatic discipleship must include that relational quality or it will be ineffective at fostering discipleship."[7] While there are a number of books available on discipleship programming, the relational emphasis cannot be overstated.

Two extremes exist when it comes to discipleship programming in youth ministry. On one hand, there is the hit and miss approach that simply puts teens and leaders together hoping that something will somehow happen. On the other hand, there is the military mentality characterized by a regimented list of requirements and duties for students to perform without any leader/student relationship.

Of course, both extremes are negligent to a point and need to be balanced. The following approaches to youth discipleship within the local church are designed to be flexible enough to include the spiritually disinterested as well as challenge the spiritually motivated.

THE CORE GROUP

I first learned about the core group concept of discipleship from two of my youth ministry mentors, Doug Haag and Eric Heard of the First Evangelical Free Church in Fullerton, California. It is largely an unstructured approach to youth discipleship which meets the social, spiritual, and emotional needs of young people.

Students of the same age and sex are placed together in a permanent core group with an adult leader who is responsible for building community and spiritual accountability within the group. Long-term ministry is established as the core group remains together throughout the young teen and senior high years. As a rule, the longer the core group leader stays committed to his or her students, the more stability and growth occur.

The chief characteristic of the core group structure is that *all* students are placed in a group—whether they want to be in one or not. The benefit of this system is that every student is contacted and cared for personally by an adult leader. This is a great advantage if you have a large youth group where kids may be lost or forgotten in the crowd.

A drawback, however, is that some students may choose not to participate in their core group. This situation not only hurts the students and restricts their involvement in the youth group, but it can also weaken the core group. In addition, individual core groups may only be as successful as their particular adult leaders. Overall, however, this structure provides interested students with excellent opportunities for group involvement, friendship, and disci-pleship.

THE INNER CIRCLE

An extension of the core group method of relational discipleship is the inner circle approach. This model focuses on a small group within the youth group or core group for additional ministry. It originated with Jesus Himself when He established His own inner circle of Peter, James, and John from within the 12 disciples.

Jesus spent extra time with these men and allowed only them to accompany Him at the healing of the synagogue official's daughter (Mark 5:35-37), the Transfiguration (Mark 9:2), and His final hour in the Garden of Gethsemane (Mark 14:32-33).

Usually in a small group setting, there are two or three students who seek additional input, challenge, and accountability. A separate, structured program isn't necessary. Allow the relationships to develop naturally, and then decide what to do from there. Perhaps it will mean simply spending more time with your inner circle of students. Or you may wish to increase their accountability in areas of personal devotion and service.

Whatever the added emphasis, be careful not to create resentment among others for which you may be responsible. But by all means, take advantage of the discipling opportunities that present themselves from within your own small group ministry.

THE CONTRACT GROUP

While the core group approach to discipling is all-inclusive, the contract approach is more targeted and structured. Contract groups are characterized by a specific duration of time (usually 6 to 12 weeks) accompanied by a specific purpose for meeting. Student participation is voluntary for those interested in growth beyond that offered by the regular youth program. Finally, contract groups require a high level of commitment, discipline, and accountability from all involved if the group is to meet its objectives.

Groups can contract to meet for a variety of purposes. Possibilities include:
- prayer and worship
- sharing and journaling
- Christian book study or discipleship manual
- Bible study
- Scripture memorization
- service and social action
- spiritual and physical training for athletes
- evangelism and witnessing

For example, a group of students might contract to meet with you or another leader for a period of six weeks for the purpose of concentrating on the areas of prayer and worship. Participants would be held accountable for attending the regular youth meetings in addition to those of their contract group. Expectations for group members might include the following:

Weeks 1–2
1. Discuss why prayer and worship are important to our relationship with God. Define what prayer and worship are.
2. Understand the ACTS model of prayer (adoration, confession, thanksgiving, and supplication) and be able to use it during group sessions and personal devotions.
3. Memorize Acts 2:42 and Hebrews 13:15.
4. Agree to pray out loud and participate in times of worship during group sessions and in all other youth group gatherings.
5. Select two praise choruses and two hymns that have special significance, and discuss their differences, similarities, and meanings.
6. Begin a personal time of prayer complemented with worship four times per week for 5–10 minutes.
7. Spend 15 minutes in prayer and worship as a group.

Weeks 3–4
1. Discuss Jesus' teaching on prayer from Matthew 6:5-13 and 7:7-11. Study the various aspects of worship as revealed in the Psalms.
2. Memorize the Lord's Prayer in Matthew 6:9-13. Memorize Psalm 100.
3. Share both yes and no answers to prayer in your group.
4. Spend 20 minutes in prayer and worship as a group. Pray specifically for the needs of the youth group, naming individuals and specific situations.
5. Increase personal times of prayer and worship to 10–15 minutes per day.

Weeks 5–6
1. In group sessions, pray for church pastors and leaders, community leaders, national leaders.
2. Identify needs from within your local community and pray for them.
3. Study and discuss the significance of Jesus' High Priestly prayer in John 17.

4. Identify the different positions of worship found in the Book of Psalms (i.e., bowing down, kneeling, standing, lifting hands). Discuss which of these positions might be appropriate during a time of worship with your youth group.
5. Memorize Ephesians 5:18-20.
6. Write a prayer to God and share it with the group.
7. Read a short book on the subject of prayer by E.M. Bounds.
8. Increase personal times of prayer and worship to 15–20 minutes per day.
9. Spend 30 minutes in prayer and worship as a group.

The preceding is just one example of what a six-week contract group might include. Use your own creativity to develop content and requirements for the groups you offer. Finally, remember to take into account the age and level of spiritual maturity of the students involved in your contract groups in order to best tailor them to your students' specific needs.

ONE ON ONE

All students have unique and differing spiritual needs. For example, Bill struggles with his parents while Carrie needs to be challenged to get involved in Christian service. At the same time, Rachel needs accountability with her personal devotions, and Neil needs to stop giving in to peer pressure.

It's simply not possible for one youth worker to minister to all those needs and concerns in a half hour talk at a Wednesday night Bible study. Knowing this fact is one thing—doing something about it is another. To meet the individual spiritual needs of your students takes an individual approach to relational discipleship. Adult volunteer youth workers are the key.

An informal way to begin relational discipleship is to have leaders take individual students into their care. Kids are looking for people to listen to them, and sometimes all it takes is an attentive ear. Praying with a student, reading Scripture that relates to the student's needs, or just sharing together can all be effective ways to minister one on one.

However, for some students, a more structured format is needed if change is to occur. Accountability is the key word as students and leaders work together for spiritual growth and change. As Athletes in Action discipling coordinator Christopher Adsit has learned, "People will do what you *inspect*, not necessarily what you *expect.*"[8]

A great program for one-on-one relational discipleship is called *Onward Bound*, described by Duffy Robbins in his book *Youth Ministry That Works.*[9] This approach is much like the contract group approach described earlier in this chapter but geared for individual students. Teens choose specific areas they would like to work on with a leader to hold them accountable. The leader and student schedule biweekly meetings to check progress on various assignments, such as Scripture memorization, Bible reading, and action tasks. I have implemented this method within the core group structure of my youth ministry with a good degree of effectiveness and student growth.

In conclusion, recognize that students are crying out for the leadership that you and your adult volunteers can provide. Begin the all important discipleship process by planting the seeds of trust, friendship, and caring in your relationships with students—then watch them grow!

THINK ABOUT IT

1. Were you discipled by someone as a young person? If so, what impacted you most from the experience?

2. How available are you personally to disciple students?
Circle your response.

Too busy   Somewhat available   Available

If you're too busy, what can you do to make yourself more available and approachable?

3. Why do you think it is especially important for youth workers to hold church youth spiritually accountable?

4. Which approach to youth discipleship mentioned in this chapter (core group, contract group, inner circle, one on one) is best suited to your particular situation and to your students? What steps do you need to take in order to begin implementing it in your ministry?

5. Think of some of the church youth you've discipled in the past. How are they doing now? What, if anything, might you do differently in your next discipling relationship?

NOTES

1. Daryl Nuss, "Equipping Disciples Who Multiply" in *Discipling the Young Person*, Paul Fleischmann, ed. (San Bernardino, California: Here's Life Publishers, 1985), pp. 182–183.
2. Robert Ricken, *Love Me When I'm Most Unlovable*, Vol. I (Reston, Virginia: National Association of Secondary School Principals, 1984), p. 11.
3. Robert E. Coleman, *The Master Plan of Evangelism* (Old Tappan, New Jersey: Fleming H. Revell Co., 1964), p. 38.
4. Tom Landry with Gregg Lewis, *An Autobiography: Tom Landry* (Grand Rapids, Michigan: Zondervan Publishing House, 1990), p. 241.
5. Gordon MacDonald, *Renewing Your Spiritual Passion* (Nashville, Tennessee: Oliver Nelson, 1989), p. 186.
6. Landry, p. 278.
7. Hule Goddard and Jorge Acevedo, *The Heart of Youth Ministry* (Wilmore, Kentucky: Bristol Books, 1989), p. 116.
8. Christopher B. Adsit, *Personal Disciplemaking* (San Bernardino, California: Here's Life Publishers, 1988), pp. 92–93.
9. Duffy Robbins, *Youth Ministry That Works* (Wheaton, Illinois: Victor Books, 1991), pp. 101–110.

CHAPTER NINE

STUDENT LEADERSHIP
AND MINISTRY INVOLVEMENT

Karl Marx viewed leadership as the struggle to win the hearts and minds of youth. Through aggressive recruitment, intense leadership training, and the high expectations of its party members, the Communist movement grew and accomplished an extraordinary amount for its cause in the 20th century. And they did it by motivating and mobilizing young people between the ages of 15 and 25.

Many forces are vying for hearts and minds of today's youth. Influences such as secular humanism, materialism, the media, the New Age movement, cults, and Eastern religions all compete to attract teens to join their ranks. And those of us ministering to

Christian teens are on the front lines of this battle.

Through Bible teaching, relationships, outreach, and Christian programs, we strive to keep our students dedicated and committed to their faith—but there are no guarantees. Many of us have experienced the pain of seeing students leave their Christian upbringing to follow other beliefs and lifestyles they hope will be more fulfilling.

I've asked some of these students why they left the church. Several of them said that they didn't feel needed or involved. It is crucial that those of us working with church youth develop their potential for leadership involvement and ministry. To ignore this important aspect of youth ministry is to deny the church its next generation of adult leaders.

WHY INVOLVE CHURCH YOUTH?

There are probably a number of reasons you may not want to, or be able to, include your students in group leadership or ministry. Perhaps they include the following:

- Reason #1: It takes too much time.
- Reason #2: Program quality might be sacrificed.
- Reason #3: It increases the chance for failure.
- Reason #4: Students are typically irresponsible with details.
- Reason #5: The church is paying *you* to run the youth group.
- Reason #6: Your students are unqualified to lead.
- Reason #7: They might do a *better* job than you. Then what?
- Reason #8: Lack of adult leadership to guide student leaders.
- Reason #9: You're not willing to share ministry duties.
- Reason #10: The Rapture might come. Why start now?

Do any of these reasons reflect your own feelings about student leadership? Now ask yourself: Are they reasons or excuses? Whatever the case, you're not alone. I've used every one of these excuses in the past, including the one about the Rapture, to avoid developing student leadership potential. But rather than dwell on the list above, I'd like to consider some reasons *for* involving youth in youth ministry.

REASON #1—PARTICIPATION VS. SPECTATING

Spectator-oriented youth workers say to their students, "You listen as I teach," "You sing as I play," "You react as I act," "You follow as I lead." What do these comments say to students? They likely think, *My input is not needed; therefore, my participation is not required.* And spectator-oriented youth workers wonder why their kids are apathetic and so hard to motivate!

In college I had a Christian education teacher who gave us a simple formula that epitomizes the result of a spectator-oriented approach to youth ministry:

$$\begin{array}{r} \text{INSTRUCTION} \\ \underline{- \text{ EXPRESSION}} \\ = \text{FRUSTRATION} \end{array}$$

To teach, plan, lead, or do anything in youth ministry without allowing students to express themselves in some manner can only lead to frustration with youth leaders, the program, and their spectator position in the group itself.

On the other hand, participation-oriented youth workers say to their students, "Here's how you can be involved in today's lesson," "Tell me about your abilities and interests, and let's find a way to use them." "Let's plan and carry out our youth activities together." "Do you want to serve in a leadership or ministry capacity? Let's explore the possibilities."

Facilitating your students' participation in your youth program and the church will not only challenge them to use their gifts but keep them more interested and motivated as well.

REASON #2—CALLED TO EQUIP

Thanks to Pacific Christian College, the words of Ephesians 4:12 will forever be etched on my mind. Painted in big, blue letters on the side of an entire wall, that verse became an ever-present reminder to those of us going into youth ministry that as teachers we were called "for the equipping of the saints for the work of service, to the building up of the body of Christ." The Greek word for service can also be translated "ministry" and further underscores the responsibility that youth workers have to train their students for leadership roles.

In turn, the young people we equip will be able to serve others as they contribute to the life and work of the church. I've found that junior high and senior high church youth are willing and eager to get involved in some sort of ministry. It's only natural that after six or eight years of *receiving* Christian teaching and ministry, some come to a point where they are ready to *give.*

Now you might be saying to yourself, *I'm not sure my kids are ready to be involved in a ministry.* In some cases, that may be true. But consider each student as an individual. More than likely you have several young people eagerly waiting to be involved in an aspect of ministry at your church, whether it's serving in the nursery or preparing a devotional for a youth meeting.

Are you providing means and opportunities to equip your students for ministry? If so, great! If not, you may be frustrating some of your more eager and capable students. I've found that these young people will find opportunities to minister on their own if none are provided. Operating on the use me or lose me principle, I've had students suddenly disappear from youth group meetings, only to discover later that they felt more challenged teaching a children's Sunday School class. Avoid putting your ministry-ready kids in a position where they can only serve outside of your youth program. Begin equipping students for ministry from within your group; then provide opportunities for them to get involved.

REASON #3—CONTINUED FAITH DEVELOPMENT
In chapter 3, I pointed out that the periods of faith development in adolescence (13–18 years) require, among other things, meaningful involvement within the faith community. Elizabeth, for instance, had attended church for years but was always on the outside of the youth group. She suffered from a lack of belonging which not only hurt her self-image but also affected her desire to grow spiritually. But one day things changed for Elizabeth. We approached her about serving with several other students in a drama ministry for children. Soon Elizabeth became very interested in making friends in the youth group and involving herself in other group activities. Her spiritual interest came alive, which I believe was a direct result of her increased involvement.

Encouraging and providing opportunities for young people to lead and minister will naturally stretch them spiritually. Lessons on working with others, responsibility, success, and failure all work to contribute to faith development.

Brandon was a member of my student leadership team. At a camp our group attended, Brandon caught some of his peers smoking marijuana in the woods. He confronted them with their actions but was largely ignored. He struggled with telling on a group of his friends, despite what he thought was right.

Brandon was a committed Christian and took his position of group leadership seriously. He eventually did what he knew was right. He came to the leaders with the information about his friends. The outcome was a very fruitful confrontation with each student that resulted in help for them, both from the youth group and their families. Later, Brandon told me that although exposing his friends was one of the most difficult things he had ever had to do, he knew he had made the right decision.

Faith develops when youth are given a chance to lead in the youth group setting. Thom and Joani Schultz note,

> Youth-based ministry provides a fertile environment for fostering kids' positive self-esteem. And a positive self-image enables young people to grow confidently as Jesus' disciples. To share their faith; to make tough moral choices in the face of peer pressure; to care for the out-cast.[1]

WHO SHOULD BE INVOLVED?

Once you determine to involve students in ministry, the next questions to consider are: Which of my young people are eligible to serve? Are there certain qualifications I should consider? Should there be different qualifications for different positions of ministry and service (e.g., student leadership team as opposed to the youth choir)? Are qualifications even necessary or biblical?

Again, Ephesians 4:12 tells us that every saint, or Christian, is to be equipped to minister. That verse includes "student saints" in your youth group. In fact, some youth leaders I know set a goal that their students will be involved in some type of ministry before the end of their senior year. Young people have great potential for effective ministry; it's not just reserved for the adults in your congregation. The Bible tells us that *every* Christian is given a special gift to be employed in the service of others within the body of Christ (1 Peter 4:10). Your students are not only called, but are *gifted* for ministry too.

Heather was a quiet and reserved sophomore when I first met her. She blended into the crowd and often kept to herself, but she was very dedicated to her faith. Before long, I noticed Heather paying special attention to the visitors who came to our group. I also started noticing that Heather would call me at home each week for the phone numbers of visitors so she could call them and invite them back. Apparently, Heather didn't feel the need to be the official youth group greeter, nor did she necessarily need my approval or prompting to do her own outreach. Because of Heather's ministry, many visitors returned to our group.

There are students like Heather in your group who are motivated, capable, and looking for a place to serve. However, not all students are ready or prepared to minister. Just because a student approaches you with a request to lead or minister does not necessarily mean that the opportunity should be automatically given. Adolescence is a time of transition and change when developmental maturity varies from individual to individual. Some students might be more ready than others to serve and lead.

QUALITIES OF A POTENTIAL STUDENT MINISTER

I'd like to suggest several qualities to look for in students desiring to step out in student leadership or other ministries of significant commitment or responsibility. I realize there are many scriptural qualities one could include in a list like this. To keep it simple (and hopefully memorable), I've chosen an acrostic of the word *minister* to suggest a few.

MODEL

To begin, look for students who demonstrate Christlike qualities in their lives. The fruit of the Spirit (Galatians 5:22-23) and teachings from the Sermon on the Mount (Matthew 5–7) provide some specifics. Students who model Christlike characteristics at school, home, and church are not only an example for their peers but can also be used greatly in student leadership and ministry roles.

INTEREST

A student's interest in a particular ministry or leadership position is another important trait to look for. It doesn't matter if the interest originates with the student or is sparked by the youth worker. It is crucial, however, that the interest be genuine. Sometimes kids want to be involved for wrong reasons—like wanting to serve with their friends for purely social, rather than ministry, reasons. So avoid pushing kids into ministry or leadership roles. Youth workers can easily talk a student into doing things he or she may not really want to do. It is always better to seek out kids who show a genuine interest in getting involved. Then you can help them find their niche and encourage them in their new ministry.

Need

Some kids simply need to be told that they're needed and will blossom once given the chance to serve. Elizabeth, whom I mentioned previously, fits this category. In almost every youth group there are those students who are simply willing to serve and are open to ministering where they are most needed. The need could be helping fold the church newsletter or working on the youth group multimedia team. As a youth worker, remember to let your students know that they are, in fact, *needed.* Encouraging students in this way might lead some to respond who otherwise would not.

Integrity

As you well know, personal integrity is a character trait that has come under fire over the last several years within the body of Christ. It is prudent, therefore, to stress to your students the importance of integrity in the lives of those who serve in the name of Christ. Honesty, morality, and truthfulness are qualities I look for in the students I involve in leadership and ministry.

Sadly though, I've also had to release student leaders for compromising their integrity. My student leaders understand that exemplifying moral purity in their dating lives is a biblical standard that cannot be taken lightly. Yet, one of my young people violated that standard and the knowledge of his behavior began to be shared within the group. It became clear that he would need to step out of leadership, not just because we needed to send a message that an immoral lifestyle and Christian leadership are incompatible, but to give him an opportunity to be ministered *to.* This incident communicated to our youth group the importance of moral purity and integrity in leadership.

SERVANT HEART

If you've worked in youth ministry for any length of time, you know that selfishness is a common character flaw among adolescents. For this reason, it is even more encouraging to observe students who are willing to develop a servant heart in ministry. I wholeheartedly agree with Charles Swindoll, who wrote, "Nothing is more refreshing than a servant's heart and a giving spirit."[2]

Students who demonstrate qualities of servanthood are encouraging, aren't they? Those who can give of themselves unselfishly have what it takes to lead and minister. It's easy to find kids to be in the spotlight. But pick up trash after a youth meeting? Forget it!

Students with servant hearts are not looking to lead so they can lord it over their fellow students. Rather, they exemplify Jesus' attitude, "I am among you as the one who serves" (Luke 22:27).

TEACHABLE SPIRIT

A teachable spirit is an essential quality for leadership and ministry. Church youth whom you perceive are willing to be taught, guided, and corrected have great potential for effective ministry. I once became frustrated with a group of student leaders because they were not participating in our group singing and worship. In fact, several were among the more disruptive ones in the group.

I decided to take my leadership team along with me to a camp where I was asked to lead worship. During the week, I admonished them to grow in the area of worship both in attitude and participation. I also challenged them to begin setting a positive example during our worship times back home. That group of student leaders demonstrated a high degree of teachability. Not only did they have a great time learning how to enjoy worship at the retreat, but they began to model worship to the rest of the group once they returned.

ENTHUSIASM

Enthusiasm is contagious! Church youth with a passion to use their gifts and abilities for the work of the Lord are not only effective but can spark your whole group to serve. Also, when young people are excited about something, they will typically give any project their all and have fun in the process. Enthusiastic students are not easily discouraged and have the ability to motivate themselves and others. Consider the quality of enthusiasm when getting students involved.

RELIABILITY

The final characteristic to look for in potential leaders is reliability. Do they follow through with tasks and assignments at home and at school? Do they remember to bring their Bibles to youth group? Are they faithful attenders at church services and youth group meetings? Do they exhibit responsible behavior? Do they have the ability to complete the things they start? It pays to ask yourself these questions when considering students for leadership and ministry positions.

TYPES OF STUDENT INVOLVEMENT

There are, of course, a variety of ways students can be involved in ministry. I have chosen to reserve aspects of service and social action as a separate category and will address those concerns in the next chapter. I have also chosen to distinguish student leadership within the youth group setting as something different from other para-youth group ministry opportunities (like choir and drama groups). The following sections will give you an idea of how to involve students in youth group leadership and suggest some possibilities for other avenues of ministry.

THE STUDENT LEADERSHIP TEAM

While the following material is primarily geared toward high school students, it may be adapted to fit junior high ministry as well. There are many other successful styles for implementing student leadership teams, but I have found this one effective.

Selection

The process of selecting student leaders is important to think through before recruiting them. For example, there is the dictator approach in which the youth leader chooses the young people he or she thinks are most qualified. This is surely the safest way to get reliable and qualified leaders. However, the students who don't get chosen are bound to accuse the youth leader of favoritism.

The second option many groups take is the democratic approach where the power of selection is given to the students themselves. Usually elections are held, and votes are cast. Unfortunately, such a process can turn into, or be perceived as, a popularity contest where spiritual qualifications may go unnoticed. Furthermore, the youth leader may be "stuck" with students who are unqualified to lead.

In selecting student leaders, I've practiced a three-phase process that balances my concern for qualified students in leadership positions and the students' concerns for wanting to be involved in the decision.

- Phase 1: Application
  1. Interested students obtain an application from the youth pastor.
  2. Two reference forms are required — one from an adult volunteer leader and another from a teacher or coach.
- Phase 2: Interview
  1. When application and reference forms are received, a brief interview is scheduled between the student and the youth pastor or an adult leader.
  2. The youth pastor determines whether or not the student is qualified to be placed on the election ballot.
  3. Any number of qualified students can be placed on the ballot, but only a certain number will be selected. Depending on the size of your group, numbers can vary.
- Phase 3: Election of student leaders
  1. Each student in the youth group receives an election ballot with the names of the nominees on it.
  2. Students are asked to consider a list of qualities in making their decisions ("M-I-N-I-S-T-E-R" qualities, along with several scriptural characteristics taken from selected passages).
  3. Student ballots are collected and counted by the youth pastor and a volunteer leader.
  4. Elected student leaders are announced at the following group meeting.

Commitment

We require student leaders to agree to the following terms:
- A one-year commitment;
- Full parental support;
- Attendance at biweekly meetings;
- Completion of various assignments, fulfillment of job responsibilities, etc.;
- Attendance at all youth meetings and youth functions.

Goals

We have five general goals for our student leaders to give them direction and guidance for leadership. These are communicated to students both verbally and in writing.

1. To grow as a disciple of Christ in personal spirituality — daily Bible reading, prayer, and worship.
2. To learn various ministry skills in order to fulfill job responsibilities and serve the youth group.
3. To learn the qualities of servanthood and practice those qualities in relationships and ministry duties.
4. To represent the general youth group population to the youth pastor and volunteer adult leaders.
5. To develop a peer ministry of encouragement and accountability with other students.

Training and Job Responsibilities

Les Christie cautioned in his book *Servant Leaders in the Making*, "Don't do anything for the youth in your group that they are capable of doing for themselves."[3] That's a good principle to follow, especially when dealing with church youth. But behind the principle is the understanding that young people need to be trained properly before they can do the job.

I suggest approaching the training process with your student leaders from two angles: character training and skills training. To develop the character traits that model servant leadership, I've had my student leaders do the following:

● Read Charles Swindoll's book *Improving Your Serve*, and participate in group discussions and assignments from the study guide.
● Volunteer for KP on retreats.
● Practice giving to others in the youth group through acts of kindness, encouragement, prayer, and letter writing.

To help student leaders develop various skills that aid in carrying out their job responsibilities, we facilitate the skills training process in several ways. First, we operate on the principle of student involvement/leader direction. For example, if a student leader is in charge of service trips, an adult leader will work with that person to help guide and direct where needed. Usually, it takes several experiences of guided leadership before a student is ready to handle the responsibility on his or her own.

Secondly, we offer Saturday training days about once every two months to teach such skills as: how to deliver good announcements and communicate your message, how to give a devotional talk and lead a guided discussion, how to delegate responsibilities and help other students with follow through, where to find resources for various games and creative gatherings, how to plan and organize a trip or retreat.

Through these training procedures, we are able to equip our students to do the work of ministry. But once equipped, students must be given tasks that are challenging, rather than trivial. In speaking of the Communists' philosophy of asking much, rather than little, from their followers, Douglas Hyde commented,

> They say that if you make mean little demands upon people, you will get a mean little response which is all you deserve, but, if you make big demands on them, you will get an heroic response. . . . They work on the assumption that if you call for big sacrifices people will respond to this and, moreover, the relatively smaller sacrifices will come quite naturally.[4]

I have always been amazed with the sacrifices school coaches can get out of students who want to play for the team. Kids who want to play readily accept daily practices, strenuous workouts, and demanding game schedules. And yet, when these same students come to youth group, we either do everything for them, or we give them real important responsibilities like turning on the overhead projector.

Challenge your student leaders to fulfill their commitments and do well in their jobs, whether they are difficult or simple. Over a year, our student leaders experience a variety of ministry roles. Some of them include:
- Publicity
- Outreach and evangelism
- Service and social action
- Creative announcements and crowdbreakers
- Visitor follow-up and visitation
- Activities, socials, and gatherings
- Trips and retreats
- Cleanup, setup, and teardown

- Fund-raisers and finances
- Teaching, talks, and devotionals

OTHER MINISTRY OPPORTUNITIES

Every student in your group can play a role in ministry. After all, you don't need to be a spiritual giant to make an announcement or staple lesson sheets. Offer different types and levels of ministry opportunities that are appropriate for the types and levels of students in your group.

The rewards of involving students in responsible positions of leadership within the youth group and the church body as a whole is well worth the effort. Here are several ideas for ministry involvement you may be able to adapt and provide for your students.

Within the youth group
- Youth choir, ensemble, or band
- Drama team
- Youth newsletter reporting and production
- Worship team instrumentalists and vocalists
- Technical team—soundboard, setup, lighting, etc.
- Multimedia ministry—videos, slide shows, photography at group events
- Prayer team
- Visitation and outreach
- On campus Bible study or Christian club
- Coordination of bulletin boards and information
- Serving under student leaders in various ministries, duties, and responsibilities

Within the church body
- Nursery work
- Children's church team ministry
- Children's Sunday School helper or teacher
- Puppet ministry
- Ministries assisting the elderly in your church
- Junior ushers
- Counseling children at summer camp
- Handbell choir
- Volunteer facilities crew

Not every student may be ready to be a student leader in your youth group, but every student is gifted in some way to serve in the body of Christ. Accept the role of helping your church youth find their gifts and encourage them to get involved in ministry!

THINK ABOUT IT

1. What student leadership or ministry opportunities were you involved in as a young person? What impact did they have on your life?

2. Are you more of a spectator-oriented youth worker or a participation-oriented youth worker? Why?

3. What opportunities are you presently providing for student leadership and ministry involvement?

4. How would you deal with a student who was in leadership and turned out to be unqualified? Check your response.
   (a) Release him/her from the position.
   (b) Help the individual work on his/her weaknesses.
   (c) Be patient and give the situation to God in prayer.
   (d) Other.

5. What benefits and blessings have you seen from equipping church youth to minister and use their gifts? Think of some specific students.

NOTES

1. Thom Schultz and Joani Schultz, *Involving Youth in Youth Ministry* (Loveland, Colorado: Group Books, 1987), p. 22.
2. Charles R. Swindoll, *Improving Your Serve* (Waco, Texas: Word Books, 1981), p. 18.
3. Les Christie, *Servant Leaders in the Making* (Wheaton, Illinois: Victor Books, 1983), p. 23.
4. Douglas Hyde, *Dedication and Leadership* (Notre Dame, Indiana: University of Notre Dame Press, 1966), p. 18.

CHAPTER TEN

SERVICE: BEYOND THE COMFORT ZONE

In my experience, no single ministry element has had a greater impact on the faith of church youth than service. Getting kids involved in serving others affects their Christian lives in knowledge, attitude, and practice. If your students haven't had much experience in service, you may find that some are initially apathetic or hesitant about serving. But be patient. Given the opportunity, students will be surprised and excited about what God can do in and through them.

Here's a sampling of responses I've received over the years from students who have been involved in Christian service and social action.

We had a great time taking Mrs. Johnson to the grocery store. She couldn't believe a couple of high school boys would take a Saturday afternoon to help an old lady out. I think we really ministered to her.

Eric, age 17 and Joey, age 17

When we first arrived, the sight of the homeless men and the smell of the rescue mission really bothered me — and it bothered me that it bothered me.

Nancy, age 16

I enjoy sharing Christ's love with the children at the orphanage in Mexico. Even though we're different in so many ways, we're all the same in God's eyes. After four years of ministering to these kids, I'm seriously thinking about full-time missions work.

Christy, age 18

At first I was scared to talk to the people at the convalescent home, but now I talk, share, and pray with them all the time. They're just people who need Jesus' love too.

Shannon, age 13

Responses like these are encouraging, but you may not get them immediately. Like anything worthwhile in church youth ministry, it takes time, effort, and a lot of prayer to develop servant hearts in the lives of your young people.

A CHALLENGE TO SERVE

It's a mistake for us to assume that just because a majority of our kids have been Christians for a long time, they understand the importance of being servants. Even after three years under the direct ministry of Christ Himself, His disciples still hadn't gotten the message of servanthood. In fact, the Gospels tell us that the Twelve were more concerned about who was the greatest among them. Remember Jesus' response? "But whoever wishes to become great among you shall be your servant" (Mark 10:43).

Let that sink in. Christians are called to be servants. For some youth ministries, service is approached as an option, rather than an essential avenue for spiritual growth and obedience. Church youth desperately need the challenge that comes through learning to give of themselves for others.

Over the years, sociologist Anthony Campolo has encouraged thousands of teens and youth workers alike to get involved in ministries of service. In his book *Ideas for Social Action*, Campolo stated,

> I believe that the church that calls young people to engage in ministry to the community by helping the poor, working for racial equality, caring for the elderly, and improving life for the disadvantaged, will find that it will attract numerous young people who are looking for the fulfillment that comes from investing their lives in the service of others.[1]

He continued,

> A church which provides its young people with opportunities and challenges for social change gives to them the opportunity to explore some of the primary reasons for their salvation. Through these activities they will come to see that Jesus is not only interested in saving them from sin and getting them into heaven, but also wants to make them into instruments through which He can do His work in the world.[2]

Powerful words! Yet getting church kids excited about service can be difficult. In most cases, knowledge is not the problem. The majority of young people and their youth workers are well aware of what the Bible teaches on service. But the desire to serve must come from within. It can't be forced; but when properly encouraged and sensitized to the importance of serving, students become more open to the Holy Spirit's guidance in the realm of servanthood.

THE COMFORT ZONE

(*Twilight Zone* music plays.)
A man with a sober expression speaks. "You have just entered a dimension of the familiar, the routine, and the safe. A place where time lingers on and growth is stagnant. You've entered *the Comfort Zone!*

"Submitted for your disapproval . . .

"First Church youth group. An average sized youth group with the spiritual depth of a grapefruit. A place where church youth are entertained, rather than challenged. Where social activities have replaced social action and consumption has overshadowed compassion. A ministry that is so *in*grown and *in*volved with its own needs that it has become completely *in*capable of *in*vestigating ways to meet the needs of others. In a word . . . *in*credible!"

Is your group aimlessly wandering in the Comfort Zone of church youth ministry? The temptation to keep God at a comfortable distance through familiar, risk-free, "don't bother me" programming is an attitudinal and behavioral rut many of us can fall into. With an obvious tone of sarcasm, Wilbur Rees described the comfort crisis I'm referring to.

I would like to buy $3 worth of God, please, not enough to explode my soul or disturb my sleep, but just enough to equal a cup of warm milk or a snooze in the sunshine. I don't want enough of Him to make me love a black man or pick beets with a migrant. I want ecstasy, not transformation; I want the warmth of the womb, not a new birth. I want a pound of the Eternal in a paper sack. I would like to buy $3 worth of God, please.[3]

Groups that provide nothing more than a "snooze in the sunshine" for their church youth need to wake up! Believe me, I realize that trying to organize a short-term summer missions trip is much more difficult, time-consuming, and chancy than simply taking sign-ups for a traditional summer camp. But the results can be well worth the effort.

Through service ministries, God can take us out of our comfort zones to places where we are forced to trust in Him. Through these riskier youth ministry situations—whether visiting a convalescent home or serving food at an inner-city soup kitchen—we come to see our own inadequacies. Then students more readily learn lessons on dependence, sacrifice, and faithfulness.

Ridge Burns underscores this truth in his book *The Complete Student Missions Handbook.*

If we spoon-feed our kids, and ourselves, on a pablum diet of safe, familiar youth ministry, we'll reap a harvest of timid spectators with delicate spiritual digestive systems. But as we challenge our kids to step out and put themselves on the line for God in Christian service, we'll stand amazed as we watch the harvest of vibrant, growing Christian young men and women come in from the field. It's more than worth the investment.[4]

Ready to go, but not quite sure how to begin? Following is a biblical model for developing a service ministry with your students, one that begins at home and will go as far as you wish to take it.

ACTS 1:8 MINISTRY MODEL

The last words Jesus spoke on earth were no doubt of utmost importance. He commissioned His remaining disciples to continue the work of ministry they had learned from Him. "You shall receive power when the Holy Spirit has come upon you; and you shall be My witnesses both in Jerusalem, and in all Judea and Samaria, and even to the remotest part of the earth" (Acts 1:8). Christ gave His disciples the mission of spreading Christianity to the world and even presented a geographical plan to follow. They were to begin sharing the Good News about salvation in Christ

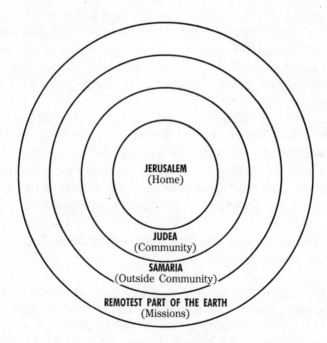

first at home in Jerusalem to their own people. Then they were to branch out to surrounding communities and ultimately the world. By reading the Book of Acts we know it worked!

Permit me to take a little license with this model and apply it as a strategy for service, social action, and missions with your church youth.[5] From the structure of Acts 1:8, the basic idea is this: Service that begins at home produces servants who will be at home serving in the world.

JERUSALEM: SERVING AT HOME

On occasion, I have come across books on student missions that suggest the best way to motivate youth to serve is to plan a "big adventure" foreign missions trip. While such an endeavor is sure to get an enthusiastic response, there is the potential for putting the proverbial cart before the horse. In other words, beginning with an event of that magnitude can be like trying to harvest the seeds of service before they've even been sown.

For example, consider the case of the man whom Jesus cured from demon-possession in the country of the Gerasenes. The man was so grateful to be freed from bondage that he wanted to travel with Jesus. But Jesus encouraged the man to remain in his own city saying, "Return to your house and describe what great things God has done for you" (Luke 8:39). Jesus encouraged the man to begin his ministry at home.

Likewise, youth workers are prudent to provide opportunities for students to begin serving at home before undertaking the big trip that often appeals to their emotions and sense of adventure, rather than a true desire to serve. Richard Foster has keenly observed, "True service ministers simply and faithfully because there is a need. It knows that the 'feeling to serve' can often be a hindrance to true service. The service disciplines the feelings rather than allowing the feelings to control the service."[6]

Encouraging your students to begin literally serving at home may not be an adventure for God in their minds, but it can be a meaningful one just the same. Offering parents a little extra help around the house or taking care of little brothers and sisters can provide fertile ground for planting the seeds of servanthood. Help your church youth to understand that if, after growing up in the church, they *still* aren't serving in this way, then maybe they need to relearn some lessons. Church youth who develop servant hearts at home by learning to give, rather than always receive, will ultimately lay a foundation for future service for the Lord.

Learning to serve at home may also include a student's immediate church family. Something as simple as stacking chairs and picking up after youth meetings or pulling weeds around the church grounds can all be ways to serve in their own Jerusalems. Or teens can gather a list of elderly people in the congregation and assist them in housework or yardwork or offer free baby-sitting for single mothers.

I believe home service will also help you to distinguish the students who truly have servant hearts. Recently I planned an exciting trip to an inner-city mission where our group was to take charge of a chapel service, singing, speaking, etc. As I expected, we had a great response. Two weeks later, however, we had a church work day and only five students showed up. (And three of them were late!) Yes, home service is often unglamorous, but it's this kind of ministry that challenges students to serve when no one is looking. Whether it's washing the church vans, writing missionaries, or simply offering unsolicited help around the house, young people who begin to serve in their own Jerusalems really learn what service is all about.

JUDEA: SERVING IN YOUR COMMUNITY

Jerusalem belonged within the larger Jewish community of Judea in the southern half of Israel. I'm also a southerner (Southern California, that is), and I consider the greater Los Angeles area to be my church's community. The next step in breaking the comfort zone and challenging your young people in service is to begin mobilizing them for social action within the community.

At this point, however, many youth ministries hesitate. Whether it's fear of the unknown, lack of experience, student apathy, or an absence of congregational support, some groups simply do not practice what they preach in terms of community service. James 2:15-16 counsels, "If a brother or sister is without clothing and in need of daily food, and one of you says to them, 'Go in peace, be warmed and be filled,' and yet you do not give them what is necessary for their body, what use is that?"

When we teach the importance of serving the needs of those less fortunate and then fail to act, are we not making the same mistake as those to whom James was writing? An episode in the life of Mother Teresa, known for her social witness of the Gospel, illustrates the importance of putting actions to words.

> Some people talk about hunger, but they don't come and say, "Mother, here is five rupees. Buy food for these people." But they can give a most beautiful lecture on hunger.
>
> I had the most extraordinary experience once in Bombay. There was a big conference about hunger. I was supposed to go to that meeting and I lost the way. Suddenly I came to that place, and right in front of the door to where hundreds of people were talking about food and hunger, I found a dying man.
>
> I took him out and I took him home.
>
> He died there.
>
> He died of hunger.
>
> And the people inside were talking about how in 15 years we will have so much food, so much this, so much that, and that man died.
>
> See the difference?[7]

What kind of a difference is your group making in the community? Over the last several years I've offered a social action program called Summer Servants. Students are selected by application and are required to give up one day per week for a period of 10 weeks to serve in the community. The mornings are spent in group prayer, devotion, study, and worship, while the afternoons are reserved for a service project. Below is a sample list of some of the projects we've done over the years:

- Serve meals to the homeless at inner-city rescue missions and participate in chapel services
- Daily Vacation Bible School in an impoverished inner-city neighborhood
- Graffiti cleanup project
- Door-to-door canned food drive
- Convalescent home visits
- Backyard neighborhood evangelistic clubs for children
- Prison visitation and letter writing
- Trash cleanup along community roadsides
- Trail maintenance in local parks and forests
- Yardwork for widows and elderly in the community
- Fixing up a local camp

Of course, this is not an exhaustive list, nor should these types of projects be reserved only for a summer program. In fact, I suggest providing monthly service projects to establish the discipline of Christian service as a lifestyle rather than a sporadic novelty. Youth missions author Paul Borthwick encouraged the same.

> The best missions awareness in a youth ministry occurs when a group (and the leaders) are consistently thinking about evangelism, discipleship, and the fulfillment of the Great Commission (Matthew 28:18-20). A one-time spurt of missions involvement may make us feel like "world Christian" youth leaders, but a year-round missions education will produce the best long-term results.[8]

SAMARIA: SERVING OUTSIDE YOUR COMMUNITY

Although the region known as Samaria was located within Israel, the Jewish people did not consider it a part of their community. Jews despised Samaritans because of their mixed Gentile blood and unorthodox religious practices. In fact, the Jewish people of Jesus' day traveled around the Samaritan border, miles out of their way in order to avoid direct contact with them.

But as is well known, Jesus did not view the Samaritans with such contempt. His discourse with the Samaritan woman reveals that He did not look down on them but rather treated them as people He could serve by sharing with them the message of God's kingdom (John 4:1-42).

Exposing your young people to a cross section of diverse people groups outside your own community can be a meaningful and beneficial service experience. First, the exposure to different cultures and socioeconomic groups can expand a young person's limited worldview. Every other month we take a group of 15 to 20 students to an orphanage in Mexico. To reach our destination, we must drive through a barrio community where people live in houses of cardboard, tin, and mud. Over the years, I've observed that teens are usually somber as we drive through the poverty-stricken area. I've also heard them discuss the plight of these people in light of their own abundance and ingratitude.

A second benefit of cross-cultural ministry is that it breaks the bonds of fear and ignorance. For example, once kids see that a young orphan boy in Mexico likes to laugh, sing, eat, play, and learn about the Lord as much as they do, stereotypes of foreigners begin to break down and are forgotten. Students learn that people are people and all are uniquely special and loved in God's eyes.

But you don't have to go to Mexico for a cross-cultural experience; the average inner city will serve just as well. Several years ago, I took a group of suburban church kids to an inner-city mission where they got a tour of skid row. Two kids literally tripped over some sleeping homeless people on the streets! After the tour, we went back to the mission and helped serve lunch to about 600 of L.A.'s homeless.

Several of the students were so impressed with the needs they saw that day that unbeknownst to me, they went back to the city the next week and passed out peanut butter sandwiches to any and all takers. They began to see the homeless and hungry as people, instead of societal problems. The following week those same students, Lisa, Juan, Matt, and Dave, made over 200 sandwiches and were joined by several other students from the group. What impressed me most was that they gave—not only their food, but also their lives. As they passed out sandwiches, the students sang choruses, accompanied by guitar, and shared their faith with those who would listen.

Whether your Samaria is a group of native Americans, the homeless of the inner city, orphans in Mexico, prisoners, or another group outside your community, strive to challenge your church youth to go beyond their comfort zones to be used as Christ's vessels to those in need.

THE REMOTEST PART OF THE EARTH: MISSIONS
It was, of course, the Apostle Paul who was originally given the divine mission of serving the Gentile world by bringing them the message of salvation in Him. Into the foreign lands of Asia Minor, Achaia, Macedonia, and Europe, Paul and his companions traveled in sacrificial service, ministering to the lost and establishing churches among them. Although Paul's personal ministry ended in Rome around A.D. 65, the call for Christians to be witnesses of the Gospel "even to the remotest part of the earth" remains with us to this day.

With an increased emphasis on youth missions over the last 10 years, literally thousands of Christian young people have gone to other countries to experience missions firsthand. However, providing opportunities for your kids to serve in your own Jerusalem,

Judea, and Samaria may be about as much as you and your group can handle right now. If so, fine. The local church needs more youth ministries dedicated to local Christian service and social action.

However, if your group is ready to go beyond your local region to do the work of ministry, it may be time for you to consider the prospect of short-term foreign missions. First, foreign missions can provide a climax-type experience for those students in your group who have been involved in service ministries year-round. While service projects and overnight trips can really make a difference in teens' lives, leaving friends and family behind and serving in another country for a period of weeks or months can stretch them even further.

Secondly, comfort zones and worldview are both challenged and expanded when church youth are exposed to foreign missions. Teens who were once overly concerned about their looks and clothes usually come back from such trips with their eyes off themselves. Also, stereotypes about different cultures and peoples are lessened as students learn to accept others the way God accepts them, rather than by what they possess or do for a living. Foreign missions trips also provide Christian young people an opportunity to reflect on their own values and lifestyles where inconsistencies are often found. When these students return from the field, making necessary changes in their own lives can be some of the most difficult, yet rewarding, results of the trip.

In addition, sending your students on a foreign missions trip allows your congregation to get involved in supporting your young people in the work of the Gospel. Unfortunately, there are some churches that do not believe students can have effective and valid ministries in missions. If your church fits into this category, then you have an opportunity to educate the congregation on the ministry and spiritual impact missions can have on the world and the lives of your young people.

In most cases, greater awareness and education concerning youth ministry and missions will generate increased support from the church. Support from family members in the form of financial assistance, encouragement, and prayer are all vital to a successful youth missions endeavor.

Short-term missions will not only help your students begin to see the world through God's eyes but may even introduce them to the possibility of considering full-time missions work.

Organization	Description
Adventures in Missions 1161 Summerwood Circle West Palm Beach, FL 33414 (407) 790-0394	One- and two-week trips in U.S. and Latin America. Construction/evangelism ministry.
Amor Ministries 1664 Precision Park Lane San Diego, CA 92173 (619) 662-1200	One-week construction trips to Mexico.
New Tribes Mission 1000 E. First Street Sanford, FL 32771-1487 (407) 323-3430	Operation Summit, seven-week expeditions into tribal settings to assist missionaries with major projects, such as construction.
SIMA/Mission to the World P.O. Box 29765 Atlanta, GA 30359 (404) 320-6090	Two-week trips worldwide for evangelism, Vacation Bible School, and construction.
Spectrum Ministries 2610 Galveston Street San Diego, CA 92110 (619) 276-1385	Length of trips can vary. Mexico outreach ministry including children's ministry, physical needs, food distribution, and construction.
Teen Missions International 85 E. Hall Road Merritt Island, FL 32953 (407) 453-0350	Eight- or nine-week trips worldwide for construction, drama, and evangelism.
Youth Unlimited Gospel Outreach P.O. Box 25 San Dimas, CA 91773 (714) 592-6621	One-week trips to Mexico for evangelism, Vacation Bible School, and construction.
Youth with a Mission P.O. Box 4600 Tyler, TX 75712 (903) 882-5591	Two- to six-week domestic and international trips for missions training, evangelism, and relief projects.

Wayne Rice, cofounder of Youth Specialties, says,

> Christianity is not in books, lecture halls, or Sunday-School class-
> rooms, but in the real world, where it is practiced and demonstrat-
> ed by those who love, serve, and obey Jesus Christ. This is why a
> missions emphasis is so important in youth ministry. . . . A missions
> emphasis gets them out of the four walls of the church and releases
> them to do something genuinely significant. They not only serve the
> Kingdom of God and fulfill the Great Commission, but they learn
> much about life.[9]

Finally, beyond the tremendous positive impact that local, re-
gional, and worldwide service can have on your students, obviously the bottom line is obedience to the Word of God. The Great
Commission isn't a suggestion, it's a command: GO!

If we as youth workers neglect to equip and challenge our students to take God's love to others, we deny our students a vital
aspect of Christian discipleship. With church youth, service to
others is particularly important because they run the greatest risk
of being ingrown, overly focused on their own needs, and viewing
the church as an end to itself. So begin where you can and reach
as far as you can—maybe even to the "remotest part of the
earth." For help in getting your teenagers there, contact the orga-
nizations listed on page 149 that specialize in foreign missions
trips for youth.

THINK ABOUT IT

1. The following Scriptures provide a biblical basis (either specifically or suggested) for Christians to be involved in servanthood:
Matthew 5:13-16; 10:42; 22:34-40; 23:1-7; 25:31-45; Mark
10:35-45; Luke 10:25-37; Galatians 6:9; Philippians 2:3-8; Hebrews 10:24. Take time to study them on your own.

2. In terms of your own youth ministry style, which person best
represents your program emphasis? Check one.
   (a) Mother Teresa
   (b) Dr. James Dobson
   (c) Billy Graham
   (d) Bozo the clown

3. List the specific projects, activities, or trips you offer within your ministry to challenge your church youth to go beyond the Christian comfort zone. Also list ideas for service you might try in the future.

What we're doing now	What we can do in the future

4. Circle the number which best represents your agreement with the principle, "Service that begins at home produces servants who are at home serving in the world" (drawn from Acts 1:8).

    1   2   3   4   5   6   7   8   9   10

Disagree   Agree

5. How would some of the parents of your church youth respond if you told them their sons or daughters were interested in going with you on an eight-week summer missions trip to Argentina?

6. Pray that your students will catch a vision to reach out to others through Christian service and social action.

NOTES

1. Anthony Campolo, *Ideas for Social Action* (Grand Rapids, Michigan: Zondervan Publishing House, 1983), pp. 9–10.
2. Ibid., p. 10.
3. Wilbur Rees, "$3.00 Worth of God," in *When I Relax I Feel Guilty*, Tim Hansel (Elgin, Illinois: David C. Cook Publishing Co., 1979), p. 49.
4. Ridge Burns with Noel Becchetti, *The Complete Student Missions Handbook* (Grand Rapids, Michigan: Zondervan Publishing House, 1990), p. 31.
5. Paul Borthwick, *Any Old Time Book 5* (Wheaton, Illinois: Victor Books, 1986). This book provides another approach to the Acts 1:8 method for student outreach.
6. Richard J. Foster, *Celebration of Discipline*, rev. ed. (San Francisco, California: Harper & Row, 1988), p. 129.
7. Mother Teresa, *Words to Love by . . .* (Notre Dame, Indiana: Ave Maria Press, 1983), p. 25.
8. Paul Borthwick, *Youth and Missions* (Wheaton, Illinois: Victor Books, 1988), p. 65.
9. Wayne Rice, "A Word from the Editor," *Youthworker Journal* 6 (Fall 1989): 1.

Conclusion

Our doctor determined that the baby would not come by a regular delivery. So much for all those childbirth classes at the hospital. Practically before my wife and I knew what was happening, the attendants were rushing her into surgery for a cesarean section delivery. We hadn't planned for it, but we were thanking God just the same that it was an option. The doctor allowed me to be present in the operating room to watch the delivery and to comfort my wife. But I think the nurses ended up comforting me more than I was able to comfort her.

I was a nervous wreck! And to complicate matters, I was trying to get our little miracle on videotape! Picture me: clothed from head to toe in sterile linen, juggling a video camera in one hand and holding my wife's hand in the other. I almost knocked down the anesthesiologist in the process!

Within only a few minutes, the baby was born. I had my son! While Lynne was wheeled into a recovery room, I was taken to the nursery to watch my new son Ross be cleaned, weighed, and measured. The maternity ward was virtually empty; and as I sat alone, staring in wonder at this precious gift from God, I was overwhelmed with love, joy, fear, awe, and humility.

Ross was born on my own father's birthday, a fact that further emphasized the magnitude of my responsibility before the Lord to raise our son according to His ways — the way my own father had. I sat in silence, praying that Ross would one day come to know his Heavenly Father, ironically before he had even met his earthly father.

Yes, it's an awesome responsibility to raise up a child in the ways of the Lord. But I know it's possible; I'm living proof. And now I'm trying to raise a fifth generation of Marian Christians (and pastor's kids at that!).

To whatever degree of success the parents of your students

have accomplished the task of raising their children as Christians, they are now asking you to take their precious gifts from God into your hands to help them complete the task. It is my hope that the information, ideas, and strategies presented in this book will help you do just that.

Remember, teens that have grown up in the church *are* different. They have their own special set of blessings and challenges. Be patient. As faith develops and grows, these kids will likely struggle through some of the issues mentioned in this book as they make their faith their own. Take advantage of discipleship, ministry involvement, and service to spiritually challenge your church youth as you guide them into a growing relationship with Christ.

My prayer for all of us, including the youth pastor that will one day influence my children, is that we might continue to faithfully serve our Heavenly Father and rely on the assurance of our salvation in His Son, Jesus Christ.

Resources

Borthwick, Paul. *Any Old Time Book 5*. Wheaton, Illinois: Victor Books, 1986.

————. *Youth and Missions*. Wheaton, Illinois: Victor Books, 1988.

Burns, Ridge with Noel Becchetti. *The Complete Student Missions Handbook*. Grand Rapids, Michigan: Zondervan Publishing House, 1990.

Campolo, Anthony. *Ideas for Social Action*. Grand Rapids, Michigan: Zondervan Publishing House, 1983.

Dockrey, Karen. *The Youth Worker's Guide to Creative Bible Study*. Wheaton, Illinois: Victor Books, 1991.

Gillespie, V. Bailey. *The Experience of Faith*. Birmingham, Alabama: Religious Education Press, 1988.

Johnson, Lin. *Bible Alive!* Cincinnati, Ohio: Standard Publishing Company, 1988.

Kesler, Jay. *Ten Mistakes Parents Make with Teenagers*. Brentwood, Tennessee: Wolgemuth and Hyatt, Publishers, Inc., 1988.

Kesler, Jay with Ronald A. Beers, eds. *Parents & Teenagers*. Wheaton, Illinois: Victor Books, 1984.

Laurent, Dr. Robert. *Keeping Your Teen in Touch with God*. Elgin, Illinois: LifeJourney Books, 1988.

McDowell, Josh and Don Stewart. *Answers to Tough Questions Skeptics Ask about the Christian Faith*. San Bernardino, California: Here's Life Publishers, 1980.

McGrath, Allister E. *The Sunnier Side of Doubt*. Grand Rapids, Michigan: Zondervan Publishing House, 1990.

Powers, Bruce P. *Growing Faith.* Nashville, Tennessee: Broadman Press, 1982.

Schultz, Thom and Joani Schultz. *Involving Youth in Youth Ministry.* Loveland, Colorado: Group Books, 1987.

Sloat, Donald E. *The Dangers of Growing Up in a Christian Home.* Nashville, Tennessee: Thomas Nelson Publishers, 1986.

Swindoll, Charles R. *Improving Your Serve.* Waco, Texas: Word Books, 1981.

Westerhoff III, John H. *Will Our Children Have Faith?* San Francisco: Harper & Row, 1983.

Wilson, Earl D. *Try Being a Teenager.* Portland, Oregon: Multnomah Press, 1982.

See chapter endnotes for sources cited.